TRADITIONAL NORTHAMPTONS[

Throughout this book, whenever the original recipe
is clear or charming, it will be left unchanged and
to indicate that it is the original form it will be printed in italics
together with its original spellings.

TRADITIONAL NORTHAMPTONSHIRE RECIPES

Food, Drink and Lore

Ian Andrews

W.D. WHARTON
Wellingborough

First published in 2000 by
W.D. Wharton
37 Sheep Street
Wellingborough
Northamptonshire NN8 1BX
Tel: 01933 222690

ISBN 1 899597 06 9

Designed and typeset by
John Hardaker, Wollaston,
Northamptonshire
Printed and bound in Great Britain by
Butler & Tanner Ltd
Frome, Somerset

CONTENTS

ACKNOWLEDGEMENTS

A large part of the research for this book was done with the help of the Northamptonshire Record Office and various libraries throughout Northamptonshire. I would like to thank all the staff of those institutions who were always helpful.

In particular I would like to thank the following:

Mrs Barton of Earls Barton for the Leek Pie recipe.

The *Evening Telegraph* for the letter on *'Ock 'n' Dough'*.

The Northamptonshire Federation of Women's Institutes for Cheese Cake, Brigstock Pickle and Jam Pudding.

Northamptonshire County Magazine for *Apple Pie*.

Major Landon (*The Pytchley Book of Refined Cookery and Bills of Fare*) for Venison Pasty, Stewed Tench, Fried Eels, Fried Perch or Trout, Oysters and Bacon, Scalloped Oysters, Strawberry Jelly, Croûtes, *Beefsteak Pie*, Plum Pudding and *To Hang Venison*.

The Trustees of the Winchilsea Settled Estates (Finch Hatton collection) for the following recipes: *Egges in Moonshine*, Pineapple Cream, Boiled Lemon Pudding, *Baked Veal*, Macaroon, *Porke Sassages*, Quince Marmalade, Hissing Pancakes, Whipped Cream, Boiled Carp, Preserved Apricockes and Damson Wine.

The Lamport Hall Trust (Isham Collection) for the following recipes: *Clotted Cream*, *Custards* and *Quebob*.

Saxby Bros Ltd. and Whitworth Bros Ltd. for photographs.

Mr K. Cheasman for help with proofreading.

Rosie Beat, a Northamptonshire lass, for appearing on the front cover, Alan Beat for the photography and Sally Tabor for the artwork.

I also wish to acknowledge the Northamptonshire Record Office for:

ZA 1507 Mrs Fermor of Ramsey – Stewed Green Peas, Fish Cakes, Tomato Jelly, Raspberries and an excellent recipe for bottled fruit and Currant Wine.

ZA 3452 Lizzie Cox's handwritten book – Ground Rice Pies, Rabbit Pie, Beef Patties and the extract from her school book.

IN 1806 Recipe book of Mrs E. Whitehead – Damson Cheese and Raspberry Vinegar.

S(T) 640 Strong Family of Thorpe Hall – Burnt Butter, Force Meat, *Strong Broth*, Friggosey and Hash.

D(CA) Dryden Family of Canons Ashby – Seed Cake, Minced Pyes, Rice Pudding, Pulled Chicken and *To Chop Chickens or Young Rabbetts*.

Where a recipe title appears in italics it indicates that the actual words of the original recipe have been used. Others have been adapted from originals.

THREE RECIPES FOR MANAGING A HUSBAND

i. "Feed him well!"

ii. "Always have a smile ready to meet him when he comes home."

iii. "Begin as you mean to go on!"

By three Northamptonshire Wives.

Taken from *The Golden Recipe Book* by Jones and Grindrod (1909)

The ford at Geddington, 1904

INTRODUCTION

Today, from Durham to Devon we select the food we eat from the same range of quality controlled, neatly packaged, buy-one-and-get-one-free, mass produced foods. We can go to our local supermarket at any time of year and get virtually anything we want, Danish bacon, Dutch cheese and so on. Supermarkets have had an enormous impact on our lives though they are a relatively recent phenomenon made possible by sophisticated techniques for the preparation, packaging and storage of food. Our ancestors did not have these facilities, and they were more dependent on the environment than we today can easily appreciate. Then they had to use each food according to its availability and each region had its own dishes that developed out of the special characteristics of the area. Northamptonshire was no exception and this book is an attempt to capture those traditional recipes together with something of the lifestyle that created them.

Northamptonshire is a super county and it is not just me that thinks this. Kings have made their headquarters here and many rich and influential families made it their home. What made Northamptonshire so desirable? It is near the centre of England and it is very beautiful but the real answer lies in the soil. Being rich in sand and gravel it drains well and that was very important in the days before the roads were made up. Particularly important is the limestone ridge. It creates a steep hill running diagonally across England from the Mendips of Somerset to the Yorkshire wolds. Anyone who knows Rockingham Hill will realize what a barrier the ridge is to walkers, let alone the poor cart horses with their heavy loads. Near the Northamptonshire village of Watford there is a gap in the ridge where it is much flatter. This is the Watford Gap well known to drivers along the M1. The Romans knew about the Watford Gap and built their 'Fosse Way' through it. Since then the A5, a railway, the Grand Union canal and a motorway have all been made to pass through it. Doubtless this is one of the reasons why Northamptonshire has become an important distribution centre.

The industrial revolution had little effect on Northamptonshire which remained a largely agricultural community and deprived of the chance to earn 'good money' in the factories many families found it necessary to work at various cottage industries to make a living. Lace, embroidered net, clocks, pottery, paper, clay pipes, book binding, carved wood, candles, brushes, dried apples and woven baskets have all been made in the county. But it was for its leather goods that Northamptonshire became most famous; parchment from Wilby, gloves from Towcester, whips from Daventry, and boots and shoes from virtually every town and village within the county.

West Street, Earls Barton

Shoemakers, or cordwainers as they were then called, were well established in Northampton by 1401 when Henry IV gave them the charter by which the Northampton Guild of Cordwainers was established. Today there are still several major shoe making companies within the county. In an area where leather crafts were so important it is not surprising that beef, milk and other dairy products were also common. The cattle were brought to Northamptonshire from Wales, Scotland and the north of England to be fattened before being sold for slaughter. The water meadows along the Nene which made good grazing for cattle also provided the willows used for weaving baskets and making cricket bats.

A few larger industries were started in the county with varying success. The textile industry became quite important, though silk and cotton weaving did not thrive. There have been several cement works, brick kilns, brewers, bell foundries and manufacturers of agricultural equipment which have come and gone but through all these changes Northamptonshire remained a primarily agricultural county.

Farm labourers were not well paid but they had access to a good variety of foods. Most farmers allowed their workers to shoot rabbits on their land and in the spring rook shoots were organised. Farm labourers often had a little land in return for their services and on this they kept a cow and various other animals. They would grow a variety of vegetables such as parsnips, carrots and potatoes, and several fruits such as apples, pears and damsons. In this sort of environment money was not as important as it is today. They had no gas or electricity bills because they had no gas or electricity and no water rates because the water came from the local well. The most important thing for them was to have enough food to live. In the summer this

Fotheringhay

was not always easy, but what about the winter? They had no refrigerators, no tin cans, not even a 'Pot Noodle' and when the cow went dry they had no milk. Methods for storing food were important to them, so milk was turned into cheese, damsons were turned into wine, beef was salted – and still they sometimes went hungry.

Not surprisingly, poaching played an important part in the lives of the poor even though the penalties for anyone caught were severe – a month in prison for poaching a rabbit and deportation for stealing a sheep. There is a record of one

Main Road, Wilby

gentleman who made poaching his sole source of income. Apparently one night he had around three hundred rabbits in his barn. These would all have to be gutted and prepared for market by the morning, which is too much for one man and it is quite likely that he had several helpers. Then, as today, professional poachers tended to work in large gangs. The romantic notion of poachers as solitary individuals pitting their wits against nature and the landowner to feed their hungry family is not totally fanciful however. There is another account of a Northamptonshire father who would go out after his children had gone to bed hungry, returning some time later with a rabbit or pheasant. This would be cooked and then the children were woken up to be fed. By the following morning all evidence of the meal had to be destroyed, even the feathers had all to be burned, because if he had been suspected of poaching the penalties could have been severe.

The working people in the town had similar food to that of the agricultural workers. The country people would come to the markets to sell their surplus. Towns were smaller then and many of the people living in them had been brought up in the country and still had country ways. Even if they only had a small yard outside their house they would still manage to keep chickens and maybe a pig. If ever an animal was suited to being kept in a small enclosure and fed on household scraps it is the pig. Pigs will eat almost anything we eat, and they are not too fussy about its freshness. The rhyme below highlights the hierarchy of edibility.

> THE BEST FRUITS ARE EATEN;
> THE NEXT BECOME A PIE;
> THE BEST OF THE REST ARE TURNED TO WINE;
> AND THE LAST PUT IN THE STY.

Pigs can get to be enormously heavy and a boar weighing a ton is not as easily handled as the cute little curly-tailed piglet of our childhood storybooks. Pigs were weighed in score (twenty pounds) so that a pig weighing ten score would be 200 lb, and they get to this size in about nine months. Killing an animal of this size or even bigger was not easy, and most people would call in their local expert who would tie the pig to a sturdy frame before slitting its throat. Pigs squeal a lot at the best of times and when being slaughtered in this way they would create such a din that they could be heard from one end of the village to the other. This gives a rather chilling meaning to the old country saying that you can use every part of the pig except its squeak. As it bled to death its blood would be collected and mixed with crushed wheat or barley which soaked it up and could then be used to make 'Hug's-pudden'. Because the offal was the meat that was hardest to store, it was the first eaten. Traditionally it was fried and this became known as 'fries'. The various parts of the pig would be preserved in different ways to keep it longer and so it was they produced a range of foods such as ham, bacon and brawn. The hocks were often used to make 'Hock and dough', which is probably the most famous Northamptonshire dish – rightly so, as it is a beautiful pie which is well worth cooking. Without the benefits of modern food storage methods they were unable to keep the meat long enough for a single family to eat it all, and it was distributed to various friends and relatives on the assumption that the favour would be returned. The following poem is from Rushden.

> HEALTH TO THE MAN WHO KILLS A PIG;
> AND SENDS HIS NEIGHBOURS FRY;
> AND AFTER THAT A LEG OF PORK;
> AND THEN A BIG PORK PIE.

The villages in Northamptonshire were not generally put on mains water or electricity supply until the 1930s, and some as late as 1950. Water would have been collected from a communal well and cooking was often done on a range or by the open fire. Rather than heat the food directly over the fire where the heat is intense, it was normally cooked at the side of the fire. A container of water placed on a trivet by the side of the fire where it would gently simmer could be used to boil up a pudding or make a hot pot. The traditional dish for which there is no recipe was the mixed hot pot. In poor households it was a matter of pride that nobody returned home without something to put in the pot even if it was only a few vegetables or a dead pigeon. It was all given to the person doing the cooking, and having brought

Northampton Co-operative Society in Abington Street, Northampton, 1910

something for the pot they would eat their fill from it. That evening the new food would be added to whatever remained and it would be kept simmering all the time the fire was alight. Foods cooked this way become so tender that even the meat breaks up in the mouth with hardly any need to chew, the flavours mingling together become mellow and delicious. This method of cooking can provide the most marvellous meals, though there must have been the occasional disaster. How it tasted and even what you got when you removed a ladleful from the pot was a matter of chance – hence the saying 'to take pot luck'. Another saying was that the pot is not at its best until the third day, and indeed it does take this long for the flavour to mature.

Roasting too was done by the fire and not over it. Roasting on a spit was only practical where they could have someone to turn the spit for hours on end. The poor person's version was to tie a piece of worsted cloth around the joint and hang it on a hook in front of the fire with a drip tray underneath and to twist it so it would keep turning first one way then the other until it was ready. So much cooking was done by the open fire that one of the Northamptonshire sayings is 'She's always got her head stuck up the chimney.' – she is always cooking.

Mill Bridge, Kingsthorpe

Without an oven it was not possible to roast food at home so anything that had to be cooked this way would be taken to the local baker, who for a small fee would put it in his oven. On a Sunday when he would not be baking bread the baker would still fire up his ovens, and people would bring him their various meals in the morning before going to church. These were collected after the service, hot and ready to eat. Typically it was the job of the children to 'run along to the bakers' while the adults walked leisurely homewards, and heaven help the child who dropped the dish, or brought home the wrong one.

Bakers had many different ways of making extra money. For example, they would sell their glowing embers to put in dicky pots. Lace makers did not light fires for fear that the smoke would spoil the painstakingly produced lace so in winter they kept warm by having a pot called a 'dicky pot' filled with glowing embers and they put this under their long skirts to keep their legs warm. A great-great aunt of mine apparently often charred her petticoats and only realized the danger when she smelt the smoke from them.

Northamptonshire had its share of poor people especially in Victorian times and later. Not many people now would want the recipe for *Tay-kettle-broth* – hot water seasoned with salt and pepper, or *kettlins* – hot water poured over bread, or even *flurrups* – the water from boiled meat thickened with flour and served as broth. A few of the more interesting but odd recipes have been included, such as making beer from treacle, but mostly you will find in this book the best traditional recipes from this county – recipes that were developed over hundreds of years, passed from mother to daughter and from friend to friend. Compared with today's ready-made convenience foods, they tend to have more flavour, and the best have that mouth-watering aroma that squeezes its way through the closed oven door long before it is ready to be served, tormenting the hungry and priming digestive systems for the treat in store. These are not just recipes from the past, they are meant to be cooked and eaten today with perhaps just a pinch of nostalgia.

All the recipes in this book have been taken from sources in Northamptonshire, and mostly date from the mid-nineteenth century or earlier. In those days when cooks recorded their recipes they often omitted quantities, never gave precise temperatures, and rarely gave cooking times. For them cooking was an art, they would add the amount of each ingredient that their experience dictated, they would change the temperature by moving the food towards or away from the fire and as for timing an instruction I like was '*cook it until it be done*'. The modern style of writing recipes is to proscribe the precise quantity of each ingredient and how it is prepared together with precise temperatures and cooking times and it has required a little imagination to do this. Nearly all the recipes have been tested but it was not practical to do this for every one, for example I did not fancy making beer from treacle, and the rook pie was made using turkey breasts. You may well feel it is necessary to change some details to improve the dishes and in doing this you are cooking with the same spirit as those cooks of olden times – you are taking your place as the latest link in that long chain of culinary artists that stretches back into the mists of prehistory.

Chapter 1

COUNTY RECIPES

All the recipes in this section have a special connection with the county of Northamptonshire where once they were commonly cooked.

NORTHAMPTONSHIRE CHUTNEY

INGREDIENTS:

4 lb (1.8kg) unripe apples
½ oz (15g) mustard
2 oz (55g) ground ginger
1 oz (30g) salt
3 cloves of garlic or 3 onions
Pinch of cayenne pepper
3 pints (1.7 litres) vinegar
12 oz (340g) sugar
1 lb (450g) raisins

METHOD: Peel and core the apples then coarsely chop them.

Place the apples together with the mustard, ginger, salt, crushed garlic (or chopped onions), pepper and vinegar in a saucepan. A stainless steel pan is best (not copper).

Gently simmer for 45 minutes stirring continuously.

Add the sugar and raisins.

Continue simmering gently with stirring until the surplus liquid has been lost and the mixture has become thick.

Pour the mixture into warmed dry jam jars.

Cover the jars and leave them to cool before tightening the lids.

If you want to be truly traditional you could stretch a sterilised pig's bladder over the jar to seal it but perhaps authenticity can be carried a little too far.

Apple trees thrive in Northamptonshire, and in the nineteenth century they were grown extensively. As well as commercial orchards, anyone with even a small plot of land would be likely to have an apple tree. A few of the commercial orchards lasted until the 1960s but have now been lost because growing apples abroad makes more sense economically.

There were several beliefs associated with apples. The best known is probably:

> AN APPLE A DAY,
> KEEPS THE DOCTOR AWAY.

A slightly more local version of this is:

> TO EAT AN APPLE GOING TO BED,
> MAKES THE DOCTOR BEG FOR HIS BREAD.

The logic behind these sayings is based on the once almost universal notion that regular bowel movements were important for good health and it was a function best performed regularly each morning. The mildly laxative properties of the apple taken at bedtime would it seems, ensure that this vital part of the morning's activities was not neglected, and all this to the financial disadvantage of the doctor. The undertaker would, however, be kept busy if the apple tree bloomed out of season according to a Northamptonshire saying:

> BLOOM ON THE APPLE TREE WHEN APPLES ARE RIFE,
> IS A SURE TERMINATION OF SOMEBODY'S LIFE.

One variety of apple that was grown in Northamptonshire is the 'Barnack Beauty'. It can be eaten with or without cooking and it keeps well, which made it a versatile variety for the one tree family. Anyone with an apple tree knows only too well that for a couple of weeks of the year there is a superabundance of the fruit. The problem is to know what to do with them. The undamaged apples may be stored but damaged ones must be used up fairly quickly and there is a limit to the number of doctors that can be kept away. All those tiny unripe apples that the tree sheds in the summer were often turned into apple chutney sometimes called Northamptonshire chutney. It has a glorious taste and can be used in many ways, with salads, as an accompaniment to pork or poultry and especially in sandwiches with grated, full flavour cheddar cheese.

STINGING NETTLE POP

'... and for me she made "stinging nettle pop", a tangy drink
of palest green, lovely on a hot summer's day.'
Like Dew Before the Sun by Dorothy A. Grimes

INGREDIENTS:

8 oz (225g) sugar
Leaves from about 15 stinging nettle plants
1 tablespoon cream of tartar
5 pints (2.8 litres) water
¼ oz (10g) yeast
Juice from a lemon

METHOD: *To prepare the stinging nettles:*

Wearing a glove, cut the stems near the ground.

Place them in a large saucepan of boiling water for 1 minute.

After boiling they loose their sting and it's easy to strip the leaves from the stem.

To prepare the pop:

Put 5 pints of water in a saucepan and get it boiling.

Add the nettle leaves, sugar and cream of tartar to the boiling water.

Place the lid on the saucepan and remove it from the heat.

Leave to cool, then add the yeast.

Leave in a warm place until it has stopped bubbling vigorously (about two days).

Strain into a clean jug. A good way is to use the sleeve of an old shirt tied at the end.

Stir in the juice of a lemon.

Pour into stoppered bottles. Drink within a few days.

This drink was often made by the old ladies. It is cheap and easy to prepare and many a grandmother would be sure to have some ready for when her grandchildren visited. She would probably be accomplished at brewing beer or wine and would have everything needed to make this delicious, slightly alcoholic drink.

Anyone who has kept a ginger-beer plant will know how to make 'stinging nettle pop', though they may be left wondering why it was necessary to go to the bother of collecting stinging nettles when there are less aggressive plants available.

The nettle had a good reputation for its healing properties and this 'pop' was thought to be more than just a refreshing drink, it was considered to be a healing and invigorating tonic.

Percy Wharton, Mary Sprake and Winifred Wharton in Swanspool, Wellingborough in 1926

There are numerous other uses for nettles. Oil was extracted from them which was used in lamps before paraffin became available, or rubbed into the scalp as a 'cure' for baldness. The juice of the nettle could be used in place of rennet to curdle milk for cheese making or it could even be used to seal leaking barrels. The leaves were boiled and eaten as a green vegetable or made into jam and could be used to pack fruit to make it last longer. It has even been claimed that when the leaves are baked with sugar they will 'make the vital spirits more fresh and lively'.

If with all this extra energy you still do not feel like chasing the flies from your larder you could hang a bunch of stinging nettles there as this was believed to keep them away and remember that all fine maidens are advised to *drink nettles in March and eat mugwort in May* if they are to have long and healthy lives.

POOR MAN'S GOOSE

(Enough for six poor men)

INGREDIENTS:

2½ lb (1.1kg) potatoes
1 lb (450g) Pig's Fry
1 large onion
Pepper and salt to taste
1 teaspoon of finely chopped sage leaves
Water

METHOD: Boil the onion, chop up fine and add the very finely chopped sage leaves.

While the onions are cooking peel and slice the potatoes (about ½cm thick) and chop the meat as described below for Pig's Fry.

Lightly fry the meats but only sufficiently to seal them.

Lay half the meat mixture at the bottom of a large casserole dish.

The new Cattle Market, Wellingborough, 1905

Cover with a thin layer of the sage and onion mixture.

Cover the meat with half of the sliced potatoes.

Repeat with one more layer each of fry, sage and onion, and finally potato.

Season with salt and pepper then cover with water.

Put on the lid and leave in a preheated oven at 225°F/110°C (Gas Mark ¼) for two and a half hours.

Messrs Gillitt & Gillitt, auctioneers, selling chickens outside the Corn Exchange in Wellingborough, May 1920

Pig's Fry is the offal that had to be eaten very soon after the pig had been slaughtered because it could not be preserved. Mostly it consisted of pig's liver with much smaller amounts of heart and kidneys in the proportion of roughly ten parts liver to two parts kidney and one part heart.

To cook the fry cut the liver and kidneys into bite size slices up to ⅜ in (1cm) thick but chop the heart into very small pieces as otherwise it tends to be rather tough. Roll the kidney and liver pieces in flour and fry all the meat fairly quickly in a little butter or lard. The result is an interesting mixture of textures with a very good flavour.

'Poor Man's Goose' is made from the same mixture of meat as the 'Pig's Fry' but the 'Poor Man' would have to be exceedingly stupid to think that he was eating goose.

BAKE PUDDEN

(Serves 4)

INGREDIENTS:
**A little dripping
12 oz (340g) boiled bacon
4 oz (115g) plain flour
Pinch of salt
2 eggs – medium-sized, beaten lightly
½ pint (280ml) milk
Freshly ground black pepper**

METHOD: Set the oven to 425°F/220°C (Gas Mark 7).

Smear a baking dish with dripping and place in the oven.

Cut the bacon into bite sized slices about 1cm thick and place this on the baking dish in the oven – do not leave it so long it dries.

Sift the flour and salt into a mixing bowl.

Mix in the eggs. The secret of good batter is to be very thorough at this stage.

Very gradually add the milk. Especially at the early stage of mixing add small amounts and mix really thoroughly until the mixture is smooth before adding any more milk. (Apologies to seasoned batter makers who do not need to be told this.)

Add a little pepper to taste. (Or try a pinch of ground ginger.)

Remove baking dish from the oven and make sure it is well greased all round.

Spread the bacon over the bottom of the hot dish and pour the batter into it.

Bake in the oven for 30 to 40 minutes. The art here is to remove it when the batter has risen and is light brown and just crisp.

Northamptonshire and Yorkshire traditional cooking have many similarities. In Yorkshire it was the sweet course that was served first because sugar reduces the appetite, so less of the more expensive meat course would be eaten. The same practice was observed in Northamptonshire where the food was served on a flat wooden plate called a 'trencher'. The sweet course was served on one side of the trencher which could not be turned over to receive the main course until the sweet course was completely finished, thus making it difficult to cheat the system by skipping the first course.

Even as late as the middle of the twentieth century it was still the practice in some country areas to serve the sweet course first. One Northamptonshire man tells the story of how, when he first went to visit his girlfriend's relatives in a village near Peterborough, he was quite concerned when they were served with only a portion of fruit pie. He ate it without comment thinking that this was all he was going to get. Then when everybody had finished, out came the main course and suddenly the table was covered with serving dishes piled high with a good variety of vegetables and meats. This happened just after the Second World War when food was generally in short supply and rationed. Here was a family that had continued growing their own vegetables and keeping their own livestock in a truly traditional way.

The recipe for 'Bake Pudden' is like a Yorkshire pudding with meat in it. It is not known which came first, the Northamptonshire 'Bake pudden' or the Yorkshire pudding but it would seem logical that the Bake pudden was first tried as a way of binding together scraps of meat to make a meal of them. Presumably in true Yorkshire fashion they made the meat go even further by not using any at all. 'Bake pudden' was traditionally made with boiled bacon – however, it is good with almost any meat, especially when served with roast potatoes and vegetables.

P.S. I love Yorkshire and its people – really I do.

ROOK PIE

(Serves 8)

*'Rooks were a great nuisance in the spring as they ate the growing corn.
Boys were employed in the fields to scare them off and farmers had rook
shoots in their own and each others' fields. Some people made rook pies.'*
Like Dew Before the Sun by Dorothy A.Grimes

INGREDIENTS: *The pastry:*

12 oz (340g) plain flour
1 level teaspoonful of sugar
6 oz (170g) lard
2 fl oz (55ml) water
1 teaspoon of salt

The filling:

1½ lb (680g) rook breasts
1½ lb (680g) minced meat
   (e.g. chicken)
3 rashers of bacon
2 large eggs
1 heaped dessertspoon of flour
4 fl oz (115ml) milk
1 medium onion
3 oz (85g) dripping
Salt and pepper to taste

METHOD: *The pastry:*

Place the water, salt and sugar in a small saucepan and warm to
dissolve the sugar.

Add the lard and allow it to melt.

Put to one side and sift the flour into a mixing bowl.

Gradually add the contents of the saucepan mixing thoroughly
all the time.

Continue mixing until the dough is smooth and pliable.

Grease a 2½ pint (1½ litre) baking tin.

Roll out the pastry and line the bottom and sides of the tin. Keep back
about a quarter of the pastry to make the top of the pie.

The filling:

Skin, coarsely chop and lightly fry the onion in the melted dripping.

Finely chop the bacon, add it to the onion and continue lightly frying for a few more minutes.

Add the flour and stir until it has absorbed all the fat and there are no lumps, then slowly add the milk with vigorous stirring and gentle warming to make a smooth paste.

When all the milk has been used add the minced chicken, salt and pepper.

Stir until the meat is cooked then take off the heat and set to one side.

Thinly slice the rooks breasts. (In the absence of rook meat try lean beef) and seal these by heating with a little fat in a frying pan.

Take the pastry lined tin and spread about one third of the minced chicken mixture over the bottom.

On top of this lay half of the thinly sliced rook breasts then another layer of mince, then the rest of the breasts and finally the top layer of mince.

Roll out the remainder of the pastry and cover the pie.

Moisten the edges of the lid with milk so it sticks to the side pastry. Make a small hole in the centre of the pastry lid.

Cover the baking tin (kitchen foil is easiest)

Bake in a preheated oven at 350°F/180°C (Gas Mark 4) for one and a half hours, removing the cover for the last 30 minutes if necessary to lightly brown the crust.

This is delicious hot or cold.

Frankly rooks are not much liked as food, the adults are not eaten because they have an unpleasant taste and are tough. The young birds have less flavour but they are not to everyone's liking and a lot of country people refused to cook them. When they are used it is nearly always mixed with other meat. Because there are so many bones in these birds the only part that is worth having is the breast. There is a special Northamptonshire way of preparing the breasts of young rooks, this is to fry them and serve them on bread.

THRUMMETY

(Serves 2)

INGREDIENTS:

3 oz (85g) pearl barley
1 pint (570ml) water
2 oz (55g) raisins
Good pinch of ground nutmeg
Sugar to taste
15 fl oz (420ml) milk

METHOD: Put the grain and water in a casserole dish.

Cover and place in an oven at 225°F/110°C (Gas Mark ¼) for two to three hours until all the water has been absorbed.

Add the milk, raisins, nutmeg and sugar. Stir and replace in the oven for another two hours.

It should have a creamy consistency.

Serve hot.

Station Road, Little Houghton

This meal is attributed to Little Houghton in *The English Dialect Dictionary* by Joseph Wright 1898-1905 (6 Vols.) though it was more widespread than just that one village. As it is made with barley seeds and water it is cheap to prepare, though it has

Midland Road, Wellingborough, 1904

to be admitted that its cheapness is more of a recommendation than its flavour, and that after several attempts I only found one person (a vegetarian) who said she *quite* liked it.

Pearl barley is the barley seed that has had the husks removed by rotating it in a spiked drum. It has the property of absorbing water well and is traditionally used to thicken stews and soups, and the slightly nutty flavour of the barley is rather tasty especially with a bit of mutton. It makes a filling meal which was widely used by poor people. Barley is mostly grown for brewing and after the harvest the women and children would go gleaning in the fields. In those days the crop would have been cut down by teams of men using scythes and as the gleaners worked in the fields the stubble dug into their legs and hands often making them bleed. The prize was free food for their chickens and a good supply of the barley that could be stored and used throughout the following year.

CHEESE

Farmhouse cheese made in Northamptonshire was usually soft cheese. The recipe below was adapted from *Northamptonshire Past and Present* Vol. 2, No. 1, p. 28.

INGREDIENTS:
> **2 pints (1.1 litres) of milk**
> **2 pints (1.1 litres) water**
> **A good handful of marigold flowers**
> **4 egg yolks**
> **Rennet**

METHOD: Gently warm the milk until it is just warm to the touch.

Boil the water and pour it into the milk. Set aside to cool slightly.

Remove the white bases of the petals and grind the yellow remainder in a mortar.

Add the egg yolks and mix thoroughly.

The milk should be warm but not above 99°F/37°C. Strain the egg yolks into it and add the rennet. Use the plain rennet and not the flavoured variety sold for making junkets.

Cover the bowl with a double layer of cloth and leave in a warm place until it will not set any more. The time required depends on the temperature but six hours should be enough in the warm – up to three days if it is cold.

Separate the whey from the curds by straining it through a cloth.

Hang the cloth with the curds in it over a bowl to drain.

Stir the curds every hour or so for about six hours. (This helps the remaining whey to be released.)

Put the curds into a press and 'let it lye a night and a day then lay it into rushes.'

The cheese was laid on a mat of green rushes for about three weeks, after which it was ready to eat.

The whey was not discarded as it was highly valued as a refreshing energy-giving drink. Whey is a sugar solution, rather like an early form of a glucose drink. In medieval monasteries it was sometimes used in place of milk.

When people milked their own cows they would separate the strokings (the first and last milk taken from each milking) from the rest of the milk. The strokings were thought to be poorer quality milk and best used for cheese-making. Each family would have their own way of doing this, probably without adding petals or egg yolks as in the Kirby Hall recipe above. There are many similar recipes to the one given above, each with its own variations, for example the particularly rich one that used cream in place of boiling water!!!

There is no famous cheese from Northamptonshire in the same way as there is from places such as Cheddar and Cheshire although we did come close with Stilton. Stilton cheese was first made about 1730 by a Mrs Orton of Little Dalby in Leicestershire and it got its name because it was sold by the innkeeper at Stilton, which is a village on the A1 just over the border in Huntingdonshire. To get from Little Dalby to Stilton the cheese had to pass through Northamptonshire and that is our only claim on this really famous cheese. However, we do have cheeses of our own such as Daventry cheese which is much like Stilton, though a little harder.

The ford at Irthlingborough

Chapter 2

RECIPES AND THEIR ROOTS

The first section dealt with recipes associated with the whole of Northamptonshire; this section deals with those recipes that are associated with a particular town or village within the county.

Unlike 'Blackpool rock' these foods do not have place names running through them, which creates a difficulty for the author in deciding which town or village to describe as its place of origin. How is a particular food assigned to a particular place when it is not known where that food was first cooked and when today it may be cooked anywhere in the country? Were Yorkshire puddings originally cooked in Yorkshire or were they adopted by that county?

High Street, Finedon, 1906

Yorkshire puddings are not now cooked very often, the true Yorkshire pudding was made using flour, milk and eggs as normal but the whites of the eggs were removed before the yolks and milk were beaten together and added to the flour. The egg whites were beaten to a froth before being added to the mixture which was then

Oundle

poured into the drip tray underneath the joint of beef that was roasting in front of the fire. The pudding swelled to fill the whole of the tray and as it did so it rose to become crisp, fluffy and having absorbed some of the juices from the meat it also had a beautiful flavour as it crunched down to almost nothing in the mouth. This was the Yorkshire pudding, a real delicacy that deservedly became famous.

There is no single criterion for ascribing a recipe to a particular place and the reasons for doing so with the eleven dishes that follow are as varied as the dishes themselves.

FINEDON APPLES

Finedon is a village rich in local history. In 1066 the village of Tingdene, as it was then known, was owned by Queen Edith who was the widow of Edward the Confessor. In 1786 a cross was erected to her memory by Sir English Dolben and this remained a feature of the village until it was destroyed by vandals in the 1930s. The Dolben family were the Lords of the Manor who lived in Finedon Hall. The obelisk that stands near the roundabout where the Addington to Wellingborough road crosses the A6 was also built by English Dolben to commemorate the good things that happened in 1789. Today Finedon is a centre for the antiques trade and has a street of antiques shops.

Church Street, Finedon, 1912

Early in the nineteenth century a baker in Finedon started drying apples in his ovens and from this developed the 'Finedon Apple', a delicacy which was to gain considerable popularity. He started with hard, sharp tasting, thick skinned apples of varieties such as 'Norfolk Pippins' and 'Beaufins' and when the ovens were only just warm at the end of the day, the baker would put in several trays of these apples and they would stay there until the next morning. When he took them out he would gently squeeze the apples without breaking the skins, which is why they had to be thick skinned varieties. The apples were treated in this way for nine or ten days until they were only about half an inch thick. These dried apples kept well and for a time became quite fashionable. Other bakers saw the success of the Finedon apple and copied it, so for a while they were made in various other places such as Kettering. Before eating they were reconstituted by soaking in water and then cooked in syrup.

One of the last of these old Finedon bakers was Berry Chapman who became well known for having a watercress bed in his back garden which he used to supplement his income still further, being listed in directories as baker, beer retailer and farmer.

Finedon

GREAT DODDINGTON ∽ CITRONELLE

INGREDIENTS: **6 lb (2.7kg) apples, windfalls may be used**
6 pints (3.4 litres) water
2 lemons
1 lb preserving sugar to every pint of apple juice
(750g sugar per litre of juice)

METHOD: Cut up the apples but do not peel them.

Put them in a preserving pan with the water and simmer until they are quite soft.

Sieve the apples until the juice has all been collected, without squeezing the apples as this makes the juice cloudy.

Discard the apple and place the juice in a measuring jug.

With a very sharp knife pare off large but thin slices of the yellow part of the lemon skin and put these in with the apple juice.

Squeeze the juice from both lemons and strain it (a tea-strainer will do) into the apple juice.

Measure the volume of the juice then put it into the preserving pan.

Weigh 1 lb of sugar for each pint of juice (800g for each litre) and add this to the preserving pan.

Heat gently with stirring until the sugar has dissolved then bring to the boil.

After it has been boiling for two to three minutes remove the lemon peel and continue boiling until it gels when tested. (Place a small sample on a saucer and leave it to cool, if it shows signs of solidifying after one minute then it is done.)

Remove all scum and pour into clean warmed jars, cover and seal when cold.

Herbert Ernest Bates (H. E. Bates) was born in 1905 in Rushden where both his parents worked in the shoe trade. He became a prolific writer best known for *The Darling Buds of May* and *Love for Lydia*. He also wrote several gardening books and towards the end of his life he wrote his autobiography in three volumes, the first of which *The Vanished World* deals with his childhood in Northamptonshire and in this he describes 'citronelle' as a preserve made at Great Doddington.

High Street, Doddington, 1919

EARLS BARTON 〜 LEEK PIE

(Serves 80)

INGREDIENTS:

The filling:
As many leeks as possible
14 lb (6.35kg) pork cuttings
16 lb (7.25kg) beef cuttings
1 packet of gravy salt

The pastry:
16 lb (7.25kg) short crust pastry

Accompaniments:
84 lb (35.5kg) potatoes
Vegetables
2 lb (900g) red cheese
5 packets of savoury biscuits
3 lb sugar (1.35kg) sugar
½ lb (225g) tea
**6 pints (3.4 litres) milk – more if coffee is
   provided!**
80 crispy bread rolls

METHOD: The day before, cook the pork and beef very slowly for a long time.

Leave to cool and the next day scrape off the fat and use this with a little lard to roast the potatoes.

The pies are made in ten big, round, flat pie tins which are lined with short crust pastry, filled with the meat and leeks and finally sealed under their pastry lid. John Ashton, the local baker, cooks these for the leek pie supper for about 45 minutes at 425°F/220°C (Gas Mark 7).

The vegetables are cooked in eight vegetable dishes which are served with the pie and a generous portion of roast potatoes. (I have quoted the figures given to me, but a pound of potatoes per person seems rather a lot.) After this course the assembly is served with cheese, biscuits and a cup of tea/coffee.

Barton has several claims to fame including the Anglo-Saxon tower of All Saints' Church which is much photographed and often features in books on architecture. This nationally famous church once had a locally famous vicar who sometimes (possibly fortified by liquid refreshment) would climb up to a ledge on the outside of the tower some thirty feet above ground, and from this platform would give his sermon to the crowd below.

For years it was a Barton tradition to bake leek pie on Shrove Tuesday and in Victorian times the whole village was involved in this communal activity. The leeks were taken to the village green where they were fed into a chaff cutter, and as they came out the ladies would catch the pieces in their aprons. Apparently they also had a trough of water there to wash the leeks which eventually were mixed with the other ingredients and taken to the local baker where they were baked. The tradition gradually declined and eventually it was kept up by the local public houses where leek pies were supplied free to all the residents of the village each Shrove Tuesday. During the Second World War this tradition stopped but it was revived in the early 1970's as part of the village's millennium celebrations and every year since there has been a leek pie supper. The recipe given above is the one that is used for that supper. It was provided by the late Mr. Horace Mills who remembered the original leek pies.

If you are ever in the Earls Barton area go along to Ashton's Bakery. They serve beautiful bread and confectionery and it is the sort of shop people travel to from miles around. John, the baker, happens to be the grandson of Elsie Clarke who up to about 1956 used to keep 'The Swan' and when, before the war, she baked the leek pies for her pub, it was done using hocks rather than pork or beef and the water they were boiled in was used to make the gelatine-rich stock which went into the pies. As so often happens the more people one asks about a recipe, the more variations one finds, however one tradition that does not change is that Barton people, but only those born and brought up in the village, are called 'leeks' because growing this vegetable was a Barton tradition and for generations here the gardeners competed to see who could grow the biggest one.

CLANGERS

(Serves 4)

INGREDIENTS:

The pastry:
8 oz (225g) self-raising flour
A pinch of salt
4 oz (115g) shredded suet
5 fl oz (140ml) water

The filling:
3 oz (85g) peas
1 medium-sized onion
6 oz (170g) back bacon
Pepper

METHOD: *The pastry:*

Sift the flour and salt into a mixing bowl then add the suet and mix.

Gradually incorporate the water stirring all the time.

Leave in a cool place.

Pitsford

The filling:

Traditionally fresh peas would be used though the modern frozen ones are excellent.

Place them in boiling salted water and simmer for ten minutes.

Chop the bacon.

Peel and chop the onion and gently fry it for two to three minutes.

Add the bacon and continue frying until cooked.

Roll the dough out on a floured surface until it is a square about ⅓ in (8mm) thick.

Mix the peas with the bacon and onion and spread over the surface of the dough. Make it slightly thicker at the edge nearest you. Spread it to within an inch (2½cm) of the edge furthest from you.

Dust very lightly with pepper.

Moisten the edge of the pastry that has not been covered with the filling.

Starting from the edge nearest you roll it up like a Swiss roll.

Gently press the moistened edge down to make it stick.

Lightly grease a baking tray and place the roll on it.

Cook in a preheated oven at 375°F/190°C (Gas Mark 5) for 35 to 40 minutes.

The clanger is a well-known local dish, consisting of a suet roll containing meat at one end and jam at the other. It was traditionally given to farm labourers who, unlike the factory workers, did not usually get home for lunch. They could start eating at the meat end, this was their main course, then they finished off with the jam end and this was their sweet course.

There were almost as many different ways of cooking clangers as there were cooks, and in the 1970s when a recipe for the Bedfordshire clanger was printed in a local paper it resulted in a vigorous correspondence about the 'right' way to cook them. Naturally each person believed that their way was the correct one.

The clanger was not only found in Bedfordshire it was also commonly cooked in Northamptonshire and here too there were many variations, for example at

Pury End near Milton Keynes there was a variety of clanger made with bacon, pays (peas) and jam.

The 'true' Northamptonshire clanger was however made in three parts instead of one. There was the meat clanger, a recipe for which is given above, a jam clanger made in the same way but using jam in place of meat filling, and the third was made from the remains of the dough which was rolled into a sausage shape without any filling. All three were baked together. Thus not only could the meat and sweet courses be eaten separately but the plain one could be kept until the following morning when it would be sliced and eaten for breakfast.

The meat clanger made with bacon as in the recipe above is quite tasty, certainly filling, and well worth trying, though perhaps you can resist the temptation to prepare extra pastry for the plain breakfast version.

Corby furnaces

CORBY ∼ CORNED BEEF HASH

(Serves 3)

INGREDIENTS:

4 oz (115g) onions
2 oz (55g) dripping or lard
4 oz (115g) corned beef
5 oz (140g) boiled or mashed potato
4 oz (115g) cooked cabbage or Brussels sprouts
Salt to taste
Black pepper to taste
1 bottle of tomato ketchup (or perhaps less according to taste?)

METHOD: Peel and chop the onions.

Fry the onions gently in the dripping to cook but not brown them.

Place the onions in a mixing bowl.

Add everything else and mix thoroughly.

Place it in a loaf tin and bake at 325°F/160°C (Gas Mark 3) for 40 minutes.

Corby was the largest of the steel producing towns in Northamptonshire and it attracted many workers, especially from Scotland. There are still so many Scottish people in Corby that it was tempting to make a few trivial remarks about the haggis being a local dish. The food which for many people is synonymous with Corby is Corned Beef Hash which is one of those concoctions made with leftovers which surpass many a more lavish meal. The recipe above was given to me by a person from Corby and when I queried the use of tomato ketchup in such large quantities I was assured that this was 'what made it' and that they would put even more over it when eating it.

NORTHAMPTON ∼ SEED CAKE

(One 12-inch cake)

INGREDIENTS:
1 lb (450g) plain flour
1 lb (450g) butter
1 lb (450g) castor sugar
8 large eggs
½ oz (15g) caraway seeds

METHOD: Mix the flour, sugar and caraway seeds together.

In a separate mixing bowl cream the butter until it is soft.

Slowly add the flour mixture to the butter beating all the time.

Add the yolks of eight eggs and continue beating.

Using four of the egg whites, lightly beat them before adding them to the mixture.

Put mixture into at least 24 cake cases and bake at 400°F/200°C (Gas Mark 6) for 15 minutes or place in a greased 12-inch cake tin and bake at 350°F/180°C (Gas Mark 4) for up to two hours.

Corby village, 1919

Books on regional cooking attribute the seed cake to Northampton or occasionally to Northamptonshire it was therefore very pleasing to come across a seventeenth century recipe for seed cake from the Dryden family of Canons Ashby and to find that it was virtually the same as the modern recipes. The seeds of the title are caraway seeds and caraway grows particularly well in the light, well drained soils of Northamptonshire. The cake contains a high proportion of eggs making it rather like a Madeira cake but without the fruit. The Madeira cake is meant to be accompanied by a glass of Madeira (the cake is named after the drink) so also the seed cake is best enjoyed with a drink such as a glass of damson wine, or at least a cup of tea.

Over the border in Leicestershire they make what they call seed cakes but these are traditionally totally different being small, flat and lozenge shaped.

Canons Ashby House

WELLINGBOROUGH ∼ 'OCK 'n' DOUGH

This is a true classic dish, cheap and very tasty and as many different ways of 'makkin it as ud fill a book'. On 6 October 1970 the *Evening Telegraph* ran an article on their readers' recipes for this famous Wellingborough dish and came up with a good variety. One letter, written in the local dialect, was particularly memorable and it went like this:

'Ow granmah uste mek 'Ock an Dough'

ALLO gal, how are yer? Did yer see the "Evening Telegraph"? Some young chap of a reporter were asrkin about "Ock and Dough" and what d'yer think he called it—a PUDDEN, and talked about mekkin it in a BAIRSON.

Nuff to mek an old gram-mah turn in 'er graive. I member 'ow I uster watch her mek it. She got out the ol' Yorkshire pudden tin, and greased it well wi' lard.

Then she lined the sides with a good 'ol crust. She put the 'ock 'o pork in the middle, then filled the tin with slices of chopped union, lumps of tater and 'praps a few chunks of parsnip.

Plenty of pepper and salt, for flaivour, and then half-filled the tin with water.

Off I was sent with it to the baik-huss, where they cooked it grand, for a penny. Course, in them days the oven at 'ome wadn't big enough four our grut tin.

It were luvly — soft crust underneath, crisp at the top. Air ol' Gramp just lapped it up—and so did us kids. I can taiste it now!

Is that the time? Slatter good, gal, and get the 'ole man's dinner. Think I'll give 'im good 'ole "Ock and Dough" for a chainge. So long, me duck.

"AIR FLO"

(MRS.) D. M. DUNKLEY
3 Burton Road,
Finedon.

Air Flo put the whole hock in and topped it up with water, making it especially cheap. Others put in just the meat, topping it up with stock. The potatoes were traditionally just cut in half, sometimes they would be strewn in with the meat. Sometimes the meat was put in the middle with the potatoes around it, while others would press them into the pastry at the side of the dish. The name *'Ock 'n' dough* seems to imply that Air Flo got it right and the whole hock was used. The jelly that comes from the hock thickens the water beautifully, and if the pie should be left to get cold it sets and can be sliced. Cold it is good, but the pie is at its best when served hot. It is a gastronomic joy from the time you first smell it cooking to the time you lean back in your chair feeling replete.

The men from Wellingborough are sometimes called 'dough boys' after this dish.

The Embankment, Wellingborough

IRCHESTER ∿ PORK PIES

(Serves 6)

INGREDIENTS:

12 oz (340g) plain flour
4 oz (115g) lard
2½ fl oz (70ml) half and half mixture
   of milk and water
1 lb (450g) lean pork
Salt and plenty of pepper to taste
2 tablespoons water

High Street, Irchester

METHOD: Rub 1 oz (30g) of the lard into the flour.

Put the remaining 3 oz (85g) of lard into a saucepan with the milk/water mix and heat until nearly boiling.

Add the warm milk to the flour and stir to a stiff paste.

Use about three-quarters of the pastry to line a small cake tin.

Fill the pie with minced pork and cover with the remainder of the pastry.

Moisten the edges of the pastry and press together to seal the lid.

Bake at 425°F/220°C (Gas Mark 7) for 25 to 30 minutes in a preheated oven (if the pastry browns too quickly cover it with kitchen foil). Then reduce the heat to 325°F/160°C (Gas Mark 3) for a further 30 minutes.

In the 1850s, the railway was built in Northamptonshire bringing with it many hungry navvies, and when the line reached Irchester the Parsons family started making pork pies to sell to the workmen. These pies became well known and were sold far and wide until they had to set up a factory to cope with the demand. They continued to be a major employer in the village for many years and in the 1920s when there was a lot of poverty they made soup which was given free to their workers and also to the poor of the village. The original pies were made from a whole side of pork from which the bones were removed and boiled to make gelatine while the meat was finely chopped and used to fill the pastry cases. After the pie had been baked and allowed to cool, the gelatine was injected into the pie through a hole in the top. The recipe above is for a pork pie that can be made at home and it comes from Northamptonshire (1909). It is interesting how many recipes there are in Northamptonshire involving pork and it certainly shows how important the pig was in their economy.

SAXBY BROS LTD

A WELLINGBOROUGH SUCCESS STORY

Saxby's, famous for their pork pies, was started by two brothers, Herbert and Edward E. Saxby, in 1904. They had both worked at the Parsons factory in Irchester which was owned by their cousins and had moved to Wellingborough to avoid competing with them. Below is a photograph taken in 1911 of the shop where they sold their pies and from which they quickly became so well known locally that they had to use a horse and cart to deliver the pies to the surrounding villages. Before long they were sending them by rail to London where they had contracts with some very prestigious shops.

Saxby's shop, Midland Road, Wellingborough, 1911

They were forced to move to larger premises and today Saxby's occupy a four acre site near Castle Fields (in which park incidentally it is still possibly to see the typical ridges and furrows of medieval agriculture). From this site they are able to supply the major supermarkets with a bewildering variety of products so when you next go shopping why not try a slice or two from those large cutting pies at the delicatessen counter, and if, when the shopping is finished, you go to your local for some refreshment, why not have a Saxby's steak and kidney pie made with ale, or if you prefer to make your own pies, then why not use ready made short crust or flaky pastry? That could be a Saxby product too.

Saxby's have stayed faithful to their roots. It is still a family business and they have remained in Wellingborough where they have created many jobs. It is true that they are always trying new products but they also continue to make the good old foods like their pork pie. Saxby's are truly a part of our county's tradition. Just go to the local pantomime in January at The Castle Theatre to watch the continuing tradition of the children (and adults) scrambling for the pork pies which are distributed by the 'Dame' and others during the 'my-side-sang-louder-than-yours' chorus.

Castle Fields, Wellingborough

LONG BUCKBY FEAST PUDDING

(Serves 12 hungry travellers)

In Long Buckby, the August feast day was a time when those friends and relatives who had left the village would make a point of returning, and when the Long Buckby feast pudding would be made. It was a clever recipe because the pudding would be prepared the day before feast day. It was cooked overnight and served cold the next day, leaving the cook free to meet old friends and enjoy the celebrations. The unusual feature of this pudding is the long time it needs to cook. It is rather like a pale Christmas pudding, and has rather uncharitably been described as very sad and heavy; however it is filling. It is easy to imagine that any pudding remaining would be given to those who had a long journey home and who no doubt welcomed its sustenance.

INGREDIENTS:

12 oz (340g) dry bread
½ pint (280ml) milk
5 oz (140g) grated suet
2 large beaten eggs
8 oz (225g) currants
8 oz (225g) raisins
8 oz (225g) sultanas
1 teaspoon mixed spice
2 heaped tablespoons dark brown sugar
2 oz (55g) dried peel
Juice and grated rind of one lemon and one large
**   orange**
2 oz (55g) castor sugar

METHOD: Soak the bread in water for two hours then squeeze out strongly to get it as dry as possible.

Place the soaked bread in a large mixing bowl, add the grated suet and pour over the boiling milk, mix thoroughly then allow to stand until cool.

Add the beaten eggs and mix thoroughly.

Then add the dried fruits, spice and brown sugar and again mix together.

Finally add the peel and the juice of the orange and lemon.

Mix thoroughly and allow to stand for several hours.

Place the mixture in a well greased tin and cover.

Bake in a warm oven at 212°F/100°C for nine hours.

Leave to cool. When cold turn out onto a dish and sprinkle castor sugar over it until white.

The Market Place, Long Buckby

WICKEN SPICED CAKE

(Serves 8)

The Wicken Spiced Cake dates back to 1587 when the two parishes of Wick Hamon and Wick Dyke were united as Wicken. After the church service to mark this event, the Rector gave cake to all those assembled, and it became a tradition to serve the congregation with spiced cake every Ascension Day. According to one account, the Rector had baked sixteen cakes, each four times larger than the one given in the recipe below. The small proportion of fruit makes this a rather dry cake but an economic one. However, the inclusion of cloves is not likely to appeal to modern tastes.

INGREDIENTS:

1 lb (450g) plain flour
4 teaspoons baking powder
4 oz (115g) butter
4 oz (115g) sugar
4 oz (115g) currants
4 eggs
4 fl oz (115ml) buttermilk
A pinch of salt
2 good pinches of allspice
½ oz (15g) caraway seeds
8 cloves

METHOD: Sift the flour, baking powder, salt and allspice into a mixing bowl, add the caraway seeds and mix.

Add the butter and sugar to the flour and mix thoroughly together.

Beat the eggs and stir these into the mixture.

Add up to 4 fl oz of buttermilk. Take care not to add too much as the mixture should be fairly stiff.

Put the mixture in a greased baking tin and push the cloves into the top of the mixture. Bake in a preheated oven at 350°F/180°C (Gas Mark 4) for 1 hour then at 300°F/150°C (Gas Mark 2) for a further 20 to 30 minutes.

MILTON MALSOR HUNDRED-TO-ONE PUDDING

(Serves 6)

The Hundred-to-one pudding of Milton Malsor is so called because it is supposed to contain one hundred pieces of potato but only one piece of meat. It is a very tasty way to make a little meat go a long way.

INGREDIENTS:

1 lb (450g) potatoes
4 oz (115g) carrots
4 oz (115g) parsnips
1 large onion
4 oz (115g) minced meat
1 pint (570ml) rich stock
Salt and pepper to taste.
6 oz (170g) suet pastry

METHOD: Peel the vegetables, finely dice the carrots and parsnips and place in boiling water for five minutes.

Cut the potatoes into small pieces add to the carrots and parsnips and simmer for another ten minutes.

Chop the onions and lightly fry then add the mince and continue heating gently until the meat is cooked.

Place the drained vegetables, onion and mince in a large basin and add salt and pepper to taste.

Pour over barely sufficient stock to cover the mixture.

Roll out the pastry and cover the contents of the basin.

Bake at 425°F/220°C (Gas Mark 7) for 20 mins then at 300°F/150°C (Gas Mark 2) for a further hour.

Chapter 3

THE BIG HOUSES

Northamptonshire is often called the county of 'Squires and Spires' but this is actually a part of a derogatory statement about the county.

> *Northamptonshire ... for more squires, more spires, more hautiness and less hospitality than any County in England.*

This is repeated here so it can be refuted. The spires and the stately homes remain but the people of Northamptonshire are the salt of the earth, easy going and friendly. How can a person who calls you 'me duck' be haughty?

Lilford Hall

We are lucky that our county is so very rich in country houses, most of which date back to Tudor times. By 1509 when Henry VIII came to the throne, the Church had acquired enormous amounts of land and treasure which went to the King when he dissolved the monasteries. He was keen to sell off the land to convert it to cash and it suited him to sell it off cheap. The result was a severe slump in land prices and the wealthy were able to avail themselves of this by purchasing large estates. It has been estimated that by the middle of the seventeenth century there were about three hundred and fifty large houses in Northamptonshire. Houses like Courteenhall, Easton Neston, Deene Park, Horton Hall, Drayton House, Kirby Hall, Lilford Hall, Canons Ashby House, Boughton House, Althorp, Abington Park, Thorpe Hall, Hinton House, Lamport Hall, Finedon Hall and many, many more. A few still have families living in them but too many of the houses became a burden to their owners rather than an asset. Understandably it was for them a matter of pride that they keep their family home when perhaps it would have been more prudent to sell up.

Today the gentry are thinner on the ground, their houses have been taken over by businesses, divided into apartments, kept as show places by the National Trust or simply allowed to decline into ruin. What were manifestations of affluence in Tudor times became insupportable burdens when circumstances changed.

Each house had its succession of cooks over the years and, in those days before the proliferation of printed recipe books, most cooks remembered their recipes - their only reference being the notebooks or scraps of paper on which their recipes were written, with varying degrees of literacy. Those that are still in existence today make fascinating reading.

Four big houses have been chosen because of their diversity and the richness of their records, these are:

Lamport Hall	home of the Isham family
Canons Ashby	home of the Dryden family
Thorpe Hall	home of the Strong family
Kirby Hall	home of the Finch-Hatton family

Lamport Hall

Lamport Hall is situated about half way between Northampton and Market Harborough and was the home of the Isham family from 1560-1958. This large and much altered house was clearly well-loved by the Ishams and is now in trust, beautifully preserved and well worth visiting.

There are some interesting insights into the Isham's way of life in the diaries of Thomas Isham which he started to write when he was fifteen. Unfortunately he did not give details of their meals, but below are a few notes about the food they ate or supplied to others and the prevalence of alcoholic beverages will surely not go unnoticed.

25 December 1671	*The poor of Lamport and Houghton came to dinner.*
26 December 1671	*The Labourers of Lamport and Houghton came to dinner.*
27 December 1671	*The more substantial inhabitants of Lamport and Houghton came to dinner.*
1 February 1672	*Bacon, eggs, wine, beer, small beer and mead.*
19 April 1672	*Bread cheese and strong ale.*
5 November 1672	*Two meat pies, a flagon of wine and mead.*

Lamport village

At the age of fifteen, Thomas would spend a lot of his time hare-coursing, fishing for carp and sometimes tench, hunting rabbits and pigeons, or shooting rooks.

9 February 1672   *Lewis killed twelve rooks with one shot.*

He also mentions bee-keeping, peaches, artichokes, crushing apples for cider, planting apple trees on his birthday and going to Northampton to eat cherries.

At that time there were several small cherry orchards in Northampton and one particularly large cherry ground which was behind the horse-fair was often used as the site for various fairs which appropriately became known as cherry fairs.

There follow some of the Lamport Hall recipes from around 1745. The first recipe is delightful – I have read it many times and am still completely confused about what it means. It is a note, probably written by the cook and no doubt it was meaningful to her.

ANOTHER WAY FOR CLOTTED CREAM

Take at night a pan of milk cream and all as it was set in the morning set it on the fire and when it is hot ready to boyl, pour it into pans as bifore and skim it the next day as the other way.

Drayton House

TO MAKE QUEBOB

Cut steaks from a leg of mutton three-quarters of an inch thick and 3 inches across or a loin of mutton cut into chops. Season with salt, pepper, thyme and marjoram minced small. Spit with large slices of onion between each piece and roast. Serve with good gravy and a little garlic.

'Quebob' is presumably 'kebab' although the dish itself is lacking vegetables other than onion and has larger lumps of meat than we would serve in a kebab, however it is excellent especially when cooked slowly over an open fire for long enough to ensure that the meat is cooked right through.

TO MAKE CUSTARDS

Take a quart of sweet cream and boil it. Put in a little mace and cinnamon. Beat the yolks of twelve new laid eggs. Fill cups and bake not too hot for 30 minutes.

When writing a modern version of an old recipe a certain amount of guessing is needed. To illustrate this the same recipe is given below in the modern style..

INGREDIENTS:

⅔ pint (375ml) single cream
2 oz (55g) sugar
A pinch each of mace and cinnamon
4 egg yolks

METHOD: Put the cream and sugar in a saucepan and heat to just boiling then remove from the heat.

Add the mace and cinnamon and leave to cool for seven to eight minutes.

While it is cooling separate the yolks from the whites of four eggs.

Beat the yolks together, then slowly add the warm cream whisking vigorously all the time.

Divide the mixture into four small oven proof dishes and bake in a preheated oven at 325°F/160°C (Gas Mark 3) for 30 minutes or until it is set.

Children's playground, Wicksteed Park, Kettering

Canons Ashby

Canons Ashby was the home of the Dryden family from 1551 to 1981 and their cousin the poet John Dryden occasionally visited them. The house which is situated on the Northampton to Banbury road is now in the care of the National Trust. It is an architectural gem which remains relatively unaltered and leaves the visitor with a profound sense of the quiet, unpretentious lives of the Drydens.

Canons Ashby House

For several hundred years it was the custom of the Dryden family to serve food in a buffet style rather than as a sit-down meal. They had TV dinners before the TV was invented! The food was served three or four times a day and it was generally accepted that the family would take what they wanted, followed by the servants. This was in no way so that the family could have the best for themselves, on the contrary there was apparently always plenty of good food for everyone. Not surprisingly the recipes from the house include a high proportion of cakes and pies as these are better suited to the buffet style than casseroles.

The recipes which follow come from the Canons Ashby of the seventeenth century.

RICE PUDDING

INGREDIENTS:
8 oz (225g) rice
2 pints (1.1 litres) milk
6 eggs
8 oz (225g) beef suet
Grated nutmeg
Salt and sugar to taste
2 tablespoons sack (white wine)

METHOD: Put the milk and rice in a saucepan and simmer gently until all thick.

Put to one side to cool.

When cool add the whites of three eggs and six yolks to the rice.

Also add all the other ingredients.

Mix thoroughly.

Wrap in a pudding cloth and boil for one and a half hours.

Compared with this the modern rice pudding is a rather plain and very cheap dish made with just 2 oz of rice, 1½ pints of milk and sugar to taste. Other seventeenth century recipes for rice pudding from other large houses were often richer, sometimes being made with cream. Later in the book there is a recipe for rice pudding taken from the Northampton School of Cookery (c1880) – see page 122. This was intended for the poor and is made with water, milk and suet.

Grove Street, Raunds

MINCED PYES

INGREDIENTS:

12 oz (340g) short crust (pie) pastry.
8 oz (225g) neat's tongue (ox tongue)
A little finely grated lemon peel
1 large hard boiled egg
1 very small apple
2 oz (55g) currants
2 oz (55g) raisins
Cloves, nutmeg and mace
Sugar
Salt
2 teaspoons brandy
2 teaspoons lemon juice
1 oz (30g) candied peel
3 oz (85g) stoned dates
1 oz (30g) sliced lemon

METHOD: *The pastry:*

A recipe for short crust pastry is given in the recipe for pork pies alternatively use ready-made pastry.

Roll the pastry out until it is quite thin.

Use approximately 8 oz (225g) of the pastry for the bases and the remainder for the tops.

The filling:

If the ox tongue has not been cooked then it needs to be parboiled.

Finely mince the cooked ox tongue.

Peel, core and mince the apple and add it to the tongue.

Mash the hard boiled egg and add this to the tongue together with the currants and raisins.

Season with clove, ground mace and ground nutmeg.

Add ¼ teaspoon of sugar and a little salt.

Finally add to the mixture 2 teaspoons (10ml) each of brandy and lemon juice.

Fill the pastry bases with the mixture.

Chop the dates and mix with the candied peel.

Take about 1 oz (30g) of finely chopped lemon, including the rind and mix it with the dates and candied peel.

Evenly distribute the date mixture over the surface of each pie filling.

Roll out the remainder of the pastry and cut out the lids for the pies.

Use milk to moisten the edges of the pastry where the tops and bases meet and pinch together to seal.

Make a small hole in the lid to let the air out.

Bake at 400°F/200°C (Gas Mark 6) for 20 minutes.

These seventeenth-century minced pyes are the forerunners of our Christmas favourite. Neat's tongue is an old country name for ox tongue, but by ignoring this and looking at the other ingredients it is easy to see how they developed into our modern mince-pies.

The Gillitt family stop for a picnic

PULLED CHICKENS

(Up to 40 sippets)

INGREDIENTS:

8 oz (225g) chicken breast
7 oz (200g) liver
Parsley
1 oz (30g) butter
10 slices of bread
Salt, ground mace and lemon juice to taste

METHOD: Boil the liver.

Allow the liver to cool then mince it with the parsley.

Add the butter to the liver and mix thoroughly to form a cohesive mixture.

Season to taste with the salt, mace and lemon juice.

Remove the breast from a cold roast chicken and 'pull it into long slips' (break it into strands).

Lightly toast ten slices of bread.

Cut each slice into quarters. These were called sippets.

On top of each sippet place a layer of white chicken breast.

Cover this with a layer of liver mixture.

Gently warm under the grill or serve cold.

This seventeenth century recipe from Canons Ashby would be just as well suited to a modern buffet as it was to their buffet style of serving meals, except that it is very tempting to update it by garnishing it with a variety of things like chopped fresh tomatoes or mushrooms.

TO CHOP CHICKENS OR YOUNG RABBETTS

This recipe dates back to the 1600s when it was the normal practice to break any animal bones before putting them into a stock. As the stock simmered the nutrients were leached from the marrow and the stock became thicker. These bones are removed before serving on sippets – slices of bread cut into shapes and toasted or fried.

Take a copple of Chickens and cutt them in peeces and chop the bones well. Then fry them with butter, and whilst they fry beate the yoalke of 3 or 4 eggs and putt in a little vinegar and sliced nutmegs and a quarter of a pound of butter and an onion and some lemon pele [and] some of the meat of the lemon. Putt it all together and when the checkens are fryed lett them stande and coule, then putt in all this and stur it well together and stray a little salt on it, then put it over a fire a while shaking the pane. Putt out the lemon pele and the onien [and the bones] and putt in a dish with some sippets.

Holdenby House, 1915

Thorpe Hall

Thorpe hall is a rather imposing house in the Italian style. In 1770 it was the home of the Strong family whose recipes are of interest because, although they are only a mere thirty-five years more recent than the Lamport recipes, they show a change in fashion. Ingredients such as barberries, burnt butter and sweet herbs became popular and the older spices such as mace, cinnamon and nutmeg were used less commonly than before.

BARBERRIES

This bush used to be common in hedgerows throughout the country but is today a rare sight because not only are there fewer hedgerows but also the barberry was found to harbour the rust fungi which can cause severe damage to wheat. The barberry came under a vigorous attack from farmers who destroyed it to protect their crops. The berry has a bitter taste especially when not quite ripe but it makes excellent jam.

BURNT BUTTER

Burnt butter was made by melting two ounces of butter in a frying pan and sprinkling in to it just a little flour. As the flour became warm it absorbed the fat. More flour was gradually added with vigorous stirring until all the butter was absorbed (this requires about 2 oz/55g of flour). They continued to heat and stir until it became a thick, smooth and slightly brown ball. This was used to thicken those sauces which in earlier days would have been thickened with eggs.

SWEET HERBS

These are sage, thyme, marjoram, savory and basil and for some dishes mint or parsley might also be included. The skill was in blending these herbs so that no one of them dominated the others yet all contributed to the overall flavour. During the summer the cook would use fresh herbs from the garden, in the autumn she would have them collected and dried for use during the winter.

FORCE MEAT

INGREDIENTS:

4 oz (115g) lean veal or other meat
14 oz (400g) shredded beef suet
Cinnamon, nutmeg, cloves, mace, pepper and
Salt to taste and ground to a powder
Sweet herbs to taste and shredded fine
1 egg
Quarter of a large loaf

METHOD: Pound the meat to a fine paste using a pestle and mortar.

Grate the bread to make bread crumbs.

Vigorously mix all the ingredients except the egg until the suet is evenly mixed in.

Add the raw egg and stir together thoroughly.

Roll the mix into balls the size of nutmegs.

Wrap each ball with a portion of spinach leaf and bake (poach, or fry) to cook.

At Thorpe Hall this was used in one of three ways:

- Rolled into tiny balls, wrapped in spinach leaf and baked, these balls could also be put in casseroles.

- Boiled then served with spinach, covered with butter, sliced lemon and barberries. (Possibly they were poached rather than boiled.)

  or

- Cut the skin of the meat and force the mix under it, bake and serve with anchovy sauce.

TO MAKE FRIGGOSEY (FRICASSEE)

INGREDIENTS:

1 lb (450g) boiled chicken or rabbit meat
½ pint (280ml) of the water from the boiled meat
¼ pint (140ml) of white wine
¼ pint (140ml) strong broth (see opposite)
1 anchovy
1 shallot
3 pints oysters
4 oz (115g) mushrooms
Whole pepper, cloves, mace and sweet
   herbs to taste.
12 balls of poached force meat balls
Burnt butter made with 1 oz (30g) of butter
   and 1 oz (30g) flour.
1 lemon
Barberries
Cocks combs or lambs tongues

METHOD: Put the meat in a large saucepan together with the water, wine and strong broth.

Add the whole pepper, cloves, mace and sweet herbs.

Then add the force meat balls and put on the heat to simmer for 20 minutes.

Put the burnt butter into a second saucepan, gradually strain the hot liquid on to it with vigorous stirring until all the liquid has been thickened.

Remove the whole pepper, cloves, mace and sweet herbs from the strained solids and put the rest in the thickened liquid.

Add the oysters, anchovy, shallot and mushrooms.

Replace on the heat for a further five minutes then serve with sippets, thinly sliced lemon and barberries.

Chopped lambs tongues or cocks combs can be added to the garnish.

STRONG BROTH

First take a leg of beef, break the bones and add twenty pints of water, a bunch of sweet herbs, onion, whole pepper and mace. Keep boiling until there are only six pints remaining then strain.

TO HASH ANY MEAT

METHOD: Cook and mince the meat.

Warm a little strong broth and add shallots, a whole pepper, mace, salt and a few sprigs of sweet herbs.

Thicken with burnt butter.

Add the meat and serve with sippets and pickle.

The Pytchley Hunt meet at Brixworth Hall

Kirby Hall

Four miles north-east of Corby on the lane from Corby to Deene stands Kirby Hall which was built by Sir Humphry Stafford of Blatherwycke. It took five years to complete and within months of it being finished in 1575 Sir Humphry died without ever moving into it.

Thirty-five years earlier Christopher Hatton had been born and after un-enthusiastically studying law he, at the age of twenty-four, entered the court of Queen Elizabeth I. The Queen, then aged thirty-one, tended to surround herself with attractive men and unattractive women. She seems pleased to have employed him as a bodyguard. He was an accomplished courtier and by 1571 he had been knighted and elected to Parliament where he became an influential spokesman for the Queen. He set about building Holdenby House but when Kirby Hall became vacant on the death of Sir Humphry he bought that house, it is said so that the Queen would have somewhere to stay if she visited him.

In those days the Queen's court was peripatetic and she visited her wealthy subjects at will. The host had no choice but to provide for the Queen and her extensive household; anyone who displeased the Queen might receive a lengthy visit from her resulting in their ruin. Only a very wealthy person like Sir Christopher would want the Queen to stay. However, he did not displease her and she did not go to Kirby Hall which remained empty for several years.

Holdenby House was completed in 1583. It was a palace eight times larger than the present building, which is enormous. By 1591 Sir Christopher had died and his debts were such that the family was completely over-stretched. They sold Holdenby House to King James I and went to live in Kirby Hall which remained in their family (later called Finch-Hatton) until 1930.

In the nineteenth century the Finch-Hattons had a reputation for entertaining their guests lavishly and their recipe books are especially interesting not only for the food recipes but also for their occasional household hints.

> *To drive away ratts or mice. Take a living ratt or mouse, burn him alive in any room whence the ratts should be driven.*

If after that you still have an appetite you might like to try their recipe for *Egges in Moonshine.*

> *Take a dish of rose water and a dish of sugar and set them on a chaffing dish of coales. Let them boyle, then take the yolkes of 8 egges new layed and put them every one from another, and let them harden and serve them up with a little cinnamon and sugar caste on them.*

The Pytchley Hunt, 1920

TO BAKE VEALE SOE AS TO GIVE IT
THE TASTE OF WILD BORE

'Take a legge of veale and bone it and lard it very well with seasoned lard, then sett it to steepe in white wine twenty foure houres with rosemary and bayes, then season it very well with halfe an ounce of pepper and halfe an ounce of ginger, and a nutmegg and two ounces of salt. Then make your pye and lett it stand foure houres in the oven, and when it is soe baked fill it up with butter. Note that you must eate it within 3 or 4 dayes after, for if you keepe it much longer it will be very soure.'

The wild boar was considered a very good animal to hunt because although normally placid it would defend itself fiercely if attacked. The bite of the boar has been described as more damaging than that of a tiger and to hunt these animals on foot armed with only a spear was a risky sport (especially for the pig). It was called heroic hunting and became a pastime for the privileged who hunted and killed the wild pig in vast numbers, happy to have it roasted and served to their guests as a demonstration of their prowess. By the seventeenth century it had been hunted to extinction in the UK and the poor cook unable to serve wild boar to the guests had to find an alternative. Above is one cook's answer.

The Willows, Kingsthorpe

MACAROON

INGREDIENTS:

8 oz (225g) ground almonds
8 oz (225g) sugar
1 dessertspoon rose water
Whites of two eggs
Rice paper

METHOD: Mix the almonds, sugar and rose water.

Spread the mixture on a metal tray and leave in a warm place for about 15 minutes to dry.

Beat the egg whites to a froth

Stir in the almond mixture.

Put the mixture in small piles on rice paper.

Sprinkle with icing sugar

Bake at 350°F/180°C (Gas Mark 4) for 20 to 25 minutes (until golden brown)

The earliest records of macaroons come from Italy but by the sixteenth century they had spread to France and it was the macaroons from the convent at Nancy that became famous. Each country had its own way of making them in their own characteristic shapes and sizes. Recipes for macaroons sometimes appear among the manuscripts of the large houses as they did in the case of the Finch-Hatton receipts. These were cooked in Northampton and they are just one of several foods which were gradually introduced from abroad especially France. The French influence cannot be ignored, many of the Finch-Hatton recipes were written in French and it reflects the fashion of that time.

PORKE SASSAGES

This was taken from the *Kirby Hall Receipts* and was republished in *Northamptonshire Past and Present* Vol. II, No. 1. p. 28. Receipts is the old name for recipes.

HOW TO MAKE SASSAGES

Take 6 pound of Porke skinned and shread very smale. Put to it three ounces of salt, an ounce of peppar, a quarter and a halfe of fennell seedes, soe much Coleander seedes, both beaten, [and] the rynde of 2 orrenges. Cut verie thinn and shreade smale, beate altogether in a Morter, then fil them and boile them a little before you sett them to dry.

INGREDIENTS:
> **1 lb (450g) minced pork**
> **Salt and pepper to taste**
> **½ oz (15g) fennel seeds**
> **½ oz (15g) coriander seeds**
> **Rind from half a small orange**

METHOD: Place the orange rind in a coffee grinder and purée it.

Now put the fennel and coriander seeds in the coffee grinder and grind them to a powder.

Clean the grinder using a few pieces of bread. These bread crumbs could easily be put in the mixture.

Add half a dozen good pinches of salt and about half that amount of pepper.

Add the pork and mix thoroughly. It is easiest to knead it by hand, like dough.

Roll into sausage or hamburger shaped pieces and grill or fry.

These sausages do have a distinctly odd flavour – how tastes change.

QUINCE MARMALADE

To make red quinces

Peel, core and quarter the quinces and weigh them.

To every 1 lb (450g) of fruit add 1½ lb (680g) sugar and ¾ pint (420ml) water.

Boil gently until the fruit is tender. The original recipe said they had to be so soft you could push a rush into them.

Turn the fruit regularly while it is cooking, the rest of the time keep the lid on the pan.

When the fruit is tender remove it from the syrup. This fruit should be red.

To make white quinces

Prepare the quinces exactly as before except boil them briskly with the lid off until they are tender then remove the fruit from the syrup.

To make the marmalade

Mix together the syrup from both boilings and continue heating it until it sets.

Allow the jam to cool slightly.

Add the red and white quinces and stir into the cooling syrup.

Put into jars as usual.

A quince looks a little like a yellow pear with cellulite. They are unpleasant raw but when cooked have a flavour like honey. They have been used in cooking since Roman times and are especially useful because of their thickening effect which makes them particularly good in pies and tarts, but of all the foods containing quinces it is the jams that are most successful. Strawberry and quince jam or apple and quince jelly are preserves for gourmets. The old fashioned quince had a property that only a few of the modern varieties retain - it becomes red or white depending on how it is cooked and they made use of this in the above recipe to produce a marmalade which is visually quite striking with its two different coloured fruits.

HISSING PANCAKES

'Pancakes and Fritters,'
Say the bells of St Peters.
'Where must we fry 'em?'
Say the bells of Cold Higham.
'In Younder Thurrow,'
Say the bells of Wellingborough.

So begins the Northamptonshire version of *Oranges and Lemons*. The recipe given below for hissing pancakes comes from Kirby Hall and is believed to date from the seventeenth century.

Take 2 or 3 eggs and beat them well, then take cream and boyle it and coule it, then stir it into the batter, then putt in more flower till it be of a good thickness and putt in beaten mace and ginger and 2 or 3 spoonfulls of eale, yeast, and a little salt, and when it has stood a little fry in spoonfulls.

WHIPPED CREAM

INGREDIENTS: **1 pint (570ml) of cream**
3 oz (85g) icing sugar
1 glass of sweet white wine
1 raw egg white
The rind of half a lemon

METHOD: Grind the rind and sugar in a mortar with a pestle.

Beat up the egg white to a stiff froth then add all the ingredients to it and continue beating. As the froth forms scrape it off and put it on a sieve in a cool place.

After about half an hour of beating you will have a lot of froth which can be served in dishes with a few thin slices of brightly coloured jelly arranged over the surface.

A pretty dish with which to end the recipes of a colourful family.

Chapter 4

A FAMOUS FIVE

This section relates each recipe to a particular individual and an odd assortment they are, a self-made businessman, a King, a civil servant, an Earl and a writer.

WILLIAM ARNOLD ∼ A self-made businessman

William Arnold's autobiography was published in 1915 when he was seventy-five, it was simply called *The Story of My Life*. Its direct style of writing described his life clearly and objectively. It is a book which puts the easy lives we have today into perspective and should be compulsory reading for all people who complain about modern conditions.

Buster Memorial, Daventry

When he was a child his mother would walk the five miles from their home in Everdon to Daventry market with a pair of shoes made by her husband. She had to sell the shoes to buy food such as sausages and then walk back again before they could have breakfast. At the age of six he was paid to scare crows from a field of barley for which he received 8d a week and a Sunday meal. He describes visiting his Grandfather where the main meal would be bacon and potatoes boiled in their jackets to save waste, and the remains of the potatoes were fried in the bacon fat for tea.

As he became older he would drive cattle to Daventry market for a local farmer and mind them until they were sold for which he was paid and received a check for as much bread and beer as he could consume. He describes going into the shoe trade where it was the custom to work until pay-day (Friday) and then start drinking until all the money had gone. It was recognised that they would not work on Mondays, and if they still had money left they had Tuesday off too. After marrying he lead a more sober life, used his money wisely and eventually owned his own shoe factory.

There is no one recipe that can be linked to him but the many little insights into nineteenth century food paint a clear picture of the way of life of the poor.

The Obelisk, Naseby Battlefield

KING CHARLES I ～ BOILED CARP

INGREDIENTS:

One carp
2 pints (1.1 litres) water
½ pint (280ml) verjuice
Rosemary, thyme and salt to taste
('a pretty deale of white salt')
2 oz (55g) butter
A pinch of sugar

METHOD: Cut off the head and tail of the fish and remove the intestines.

Place the fish in a large saucepan and cover with water and verjuice.

Add the herbs and salt and leave to boil for at least 30 minutes.

When the fish is cooked remove the scum from the broth.

Take 3 fl oz of the broth add a pinch of sugar and the butter.

Blend these together by beating as thoroughly as possible.

Remove the fish from the saucepan and lay on a dish, and pour the sauce on it.

King Charles I came to the throne in 1625 and ruled for twenty years during which time he amassed enormous debts and illegally levied tonnage and poundage. He was disliked by some people for his high church views and by others for his arrogance. When he had to fight to keep his throne he had difficulty getting sufficient soldiers and it was here in Northamptonshire, just outside the village of Naseby, that on 14 June 1645 his troops were defeated by Cromwell's army

The recipe above comes from the Kirby Hall receipts where it was said to be how Charles I *'had his Carpes dresd'*. The recipe calls for the use of verjuice which was the juice of unripe apples or grapes (depending on the season) which had been stored and become rather vinegary. Verjuice was very widely used in medieval recipes but is not available today, a substitute for it is to mix ¾ pint of apple juice with ¼ pint of cider vinegar and the juice of a lemon.

SAMUEL PEPYS ∿ VENISON PASTY

INGREDIENTS:

2 lb (900g) loin of venison
Salt, pepper and ground nutmeg
1 lb (450g) short crust pastry
Shredded beef suet
1 egg
Stock to serve

METHOD: Place the meat in boiling water for at least 15 minutes.

Remove the meat and beat it into a paste.

Season the paste with salt, pepper and a pinch of nutmeg. This is the filling.

Use ½ lb of short crust pastry for every 1 lb of filling.

Roll half of the pastry into a 7 inch (18cm) square.

Sprinkle lightly with shredded beef suet.

Place the filling in the centre and spread out until about 1 inch (2½cm) thick. Do not cover the pastry right up to the edge.

Roll out the remainder of the pastry as before and cover the filling.

Brush the edges of the pastry with beaten egg and pinch together to seal.

Bake at 425°F/220°C (Gas Mark 7) for 40 minutes. Serve with a good stock.

Samuel Pepys lived in Huntingdonshire but he occasionally visited our county as, for example, on 12 October 1660 when he recorded dining on venison pasty. Clearly in those days venison was a reasonably common meat but since then the steady decline of our woodland has reduced the population of indigenous deer which have also suffered because of competition with smaller species which have been introduced, such as the muntjak.

Five thousand years ago virtually the whole of Northamptonshire was covered by woodland. Gradually the woods were cleared but they were still fairly extensive in Tudor times. The ownership of woodlands and the right to hunt there was in those days a very complex matter. Typically they were owned by the King who employed several men to take care of them. Only these men and some of the local gentry would have had hunting rights but if an animal strayed out of the wood it could then be killed by anyone. It seems that 'straying out of the wood' was sometimes interpreted in rather imaginative ways and no doubt many a deer was driven out of the woodland before being killed. At least one Northamptonshire man was hanged after he was discovered taking a deer home. The trail of blood and damaged vegetation where he had dragged the carcass from the wood had all too clearly disproved his claim that it had been killed outside the woods.

Today if you buy venison it will probably have come from a deer farm.

Rothwell Fair

EARL SPENCER ∼ STEWED TENCH

John Spencer, a sheep farmer from Warwickshire moved to Althorp in 1508 and bought the estate which has since become the Spencer family home. His descendants include George Washington, Winston Spencer Churchill and Diana, Princess of Wales. The recipe that follows is for stewed tench is dated about 1815 and was a favourite of the then Earl.

Althorp House

INGREDIENTS:	One fish per person
	½ pint (280ml) white wine
	¼ pint (140ml) claret
	¼ pint (140ml) water
	One onion
	1 oz (30g) horseradish root
	12 anchovies
	Salt, pepper, mace, ginger and a few cloves
	1 oz (30g) butter
	2 tablespoons of flour

METHOD: Carefully scrape the skin of the fish to clean it.

Remove the head and intestines from each fish and carefully fillet it.

Place the fish in a stew pan (or a large saucepan with a lid).

Cover the fish with the wine, claret and water.

Finely chop the onion and add this to the fish.

Add the ground ginger, salt, pepper, ground mace and cloves.

Grate the horseradish into the stew pan and simmer for 30 minutes.

Add the anchovies and simmer for another ten minutes.

Remove the fish and keep it in a warm place.

Melt the butter in a frying pan and mix in the flour until it is smooth.

Slowly add the liquid to the flour with vigorous stirring.

Serve the fish with the thickened sauce poured over it.

The Lake, Althorp Park

H. E. BATES

The local writer Herbert Bates was born in Rushden and his autobiography *The Vanished World* describes beautifully his life as a *bwoy chap* there.

Rushden Parade, 1906

He describes taking tea in an enamelled can to his father in the shoe factory where he worked and also visiting relatives around the time of the first world war where they ate well. A good meal had a main course of steak and kidney pie, rabbit pie or beef pudding served with potatoes and carrots, peas or beans, followed by a sweet course of apple pie or plum pie. For tea they would have bread and butter with plum or damson jam followed by dough cake or caraway cake. He refers to 'biznins' which was made with *beestings*, the first milk from the cow after the birth of its calf which is thick and yellow rather like raw egg yolk. It was watered down two or three times before being cooked into a creamy thick egg custard. It was customary for a farmer to send a jug of beestings to a friend, but the jug must not be returned empty because that meant bad luck for the calf. (It would certainly have been bad luck for the farmer.) Bates also described the *diar drink* (normally spelt dea or dia) as being like watered down vermouth. It is a herb beer made with dead nettles (dea nettles), dandelions and root ginger.

At the age of sixteen Bates left school and went to work as a clerk in a leather factory and it was in his spare time here that he wrote his first published novel *The Two Sisters* for which he received £25 and an entrée into the literary world. His autobiography describes beautifully his life in Rushden in those days before fish fingers and beefburgers.

The Avenue, Rushden Hall

Chapter 5

DRINKS

BEER

Beer and bread have been extensively produced throughout British history. When the Romans invaded Britain they were sustained by these two products of fermentation and when Abbot Ralph of Crowland Abbey visited Wellingborough in 1253 he and his retinue consumed one cow, fifty-nine pigs, two hundred and sixty pigeons, seventy-two hens, twenty-five geese, five cheeses and, of course, huge quantities of bread and beer. In 1645 when Cromwell visited the same town and stationed his troops there before the battle of Naseby it was bread and beer that sustained them too, at the cost of ¼d per pint (nearly a thousand pints of beer for a pound!!!).

Croyland Farm, Wellingborough

Brewing beer is an ancient art especially in the monasteries where brewing techniques were studied and greatly improved. Right into the nineteenth century it was common practice for the beer to be brewed on a relatively small scale, often on the farms where the barley had been grown. It was the farmer's wife who was usually responsible for producing it and while employed in this task she would be excused all other household duties. It was an important task. If it was successful it could provide them with a good income and it was expected of the farmer that he should supply beer for his labourers especially during the long weeks of harvest. It was the custom in Northamptonshire to make the sign of the cross over the brew when setting it up in order to ensure the quality of the product. Gradually breweries took over the mass production of beer. Initially they did so on a local scale, but gradually as transport improved they developed the sophisticated distribution networks we see today.

OTHER DRINKS

Wine was made from a wide range of vegetables and fruits, particularly popular were parsnips, potatoes, currants and apples which were also used to make that ever popular drink, cider. See also in this book the cattern bowl and stinging nettle pop. Alcoholic drinks were very commonly consumed, because other than milk and water they had very little to drink that was not alcoholic. Tisanes could be made by pouring boiling water over a few leaves or petals such as camomile, scented rose petals or bramble leaves.

Eydon stocks, 1905

BEER MADE FROM TREACLE

In 1757 there was a severe shortage of wheat to the extent that on the Eighth of November in that year Dr James Stonehouse of Northampton felt it necessary to write an article in the *Northamptonshire Mercury* suggesting recipes designed to help the poor. One of these recipes was for beer made from treacle. There is a similar drink called *metheglin* (pronounced methegle) which in Northamptonshire was a sort of beer made using the remains of the honeycomb after the honey had been extracted.

INGREDIENTS:
2 gallons (9 litres) boiling water
1 lb (450g) treacle
¼ oz (10g) ginger
2 Bay leaves

METHOD: Boil all three ingredients together for 15 minutes then remove the ginger and the bay leaves.

Allow to cool then add the yeast then proceed as for brewing beer.

DAMSON WINE

INGREDIENTS:
6 lb (2.7kg) damsons
1 gallon (4.5 litres) water
3 lb (1.35kg) brown sugar
⅛ oz (3.5g) isinglass
½ pint (280ml) brandy

METHOD: Choose ripe damsons, put them into a two-gallon container, add the water   and leave them to stand for eight days stirring every day.

Strain the fruit juice into a barrel through a fine sieve and keep the stones.

To every gallon of liquid add 3 lb (1.35kg) of brown sugar and stir until dissolved.

Add the yeast and let it stand for 12 hours.

Wash and crack the stones then place them in the barrel with the wine.

Loosely stopper the barrel until it stops working, this takes several days, then stopper it tightly and leave to stand for five to six months.

Pour the wine into a clean container without disturbing the sediment.

Add ⅛ oz (3.5g) of isinglass and half a bottle of brandy then stir and stopper.

Leave for a day to settle.

Swill a little brandy into each bottle to sterilise it then pour in the clear wine, cork tightly and seal with melted wax.

Damsons grow in slightly wetter conditions than plums and were better suited to the Northamptonshire climate. They make particularly good wine and jam so it is not surprising that there are several recipes for these two products in the county archives. The recipe above came from the Finch-Hatton manuscripts c1817.

In Northamptonshire it was traditional for home brewers to ferment wine in open earthenware vessels called pancheons. A pancheon was made of a coarse pottery similar to that used for flower pots but they were shaped rather like a large fruit bowl with flared sides. It was glazed often only on the inside. With its wide spreading top it was ideal for stopping the froth bubbling over as the yeast fermented. During this stage a clean cloth would be placed over the brew to reduce the chances of contamination and as long as there was a head of froth on it the wine would not turn to vinegar. As soon as the fermentation slowed and before the head became too thin they had to transfer it to a sealed container, making sure that the sediment was left behind. It was put in an earthenware jar which could be loosely stoppered with a cork and then left to finish its fermentation. When this was complete the clear liquid was bottled, once again making sure the sediment was left behind. Fermentation would be stopped at this stage by the addition of distilled wine with a much higher alcohol content. At their best these wines were very good but they were prone to contamination and the results were probably less consistent than when an expert uses modern home-brewing techniques. The pancheon was heavy and once full could not be moved easily. Being made of pottery they were easily broken and if a Northamptonshire person wanted to tell someone they were useless they might have said 'You're about as much use as a cracked pancheon.'

SMALL MEAD

Sometimes wine was deliberately made rather weak and this was known as small wine. Below is a recipe for small mead.

INGREDIENTS:

1 gallon (4.5 litres) water
21 oz (600g) honey
5 oz (140g) sugar
½ lemon
2 cloves
Yeast

METHOD: Boil the water, honey and sugar together for half an hour taking off the scum as necessary.

While it is still hot put the liquid into an earthenware cask together with the cloves and the peel and juice of half a lemon.

Allow the liquid to cool then add the yeast and lightly stopper the cask.

Leave the mead in the cask for eight days then decant it into bottles which are then tightly corked.

This would have been drunk fairly soon after bottling as it does not keep for long periods of time.

Higham Ferrers Feast, 1908

MEAD

Mead is an ancient drink in this country probably predating beer or ale. The nineteenth century recipe from which this was taken recommended using brandy to stop the fermentation but probably this would have been a distilled wine rather than the fine quality drink we call brandy. Anyone trying this recipe might prefer to stop the fermentation using vodka as this will not adversely affect the flavour of the mead.

INGREDIENTS:

5 lb (2.25kg) honey
5 pints (2.8 litres) of water
3 lemons
Yeast
½ bottle of vodka

METHOD: Boil the water and honey together then add the rind and juice of three lemons.

While still hot pour into a sterile barrel and leave to cool, then add the yeast.

Stopper loosely and leave in a warm place to ferment.

Decant the wine into a sterile container taking care not to disturb the sediment, add the vodka and stopper tightly.

Leave to settle and when the wine is clear bottle in the usual way.

SPICED MEAD

This is another nineteenth century version of mead. Imagine a small group of people sitting in front of an open fire on a cold winter's night with only the firelight and a couple of candles to illuminate the room. They may be joking about the day's events or perhaps telling stories about 'the good old days', with the fire warming them on the outside and the spiced mead warming them on the inside. It was very much a winter drink made in exactly the same way as mead above except that the boiling water would have placed in it ½ oz (15g) of well bruised root ginger, six cloves and cinnamon or nutmeg to taste.

GINGER WINE

INGREDIENTS:

3 gallons (13.5 litres) water
15 lb (6.75kg) sugar
5 oz (142g) ginger well bruised
4 lemons
2½ lb (1.1kg) raisins
3 teaspoons yeast
1½ pints (850ml) brandy

METHOD: Boil the ingredients together for an hour, skimming off the scum as necessary.

While still hot add the juice and peel of the lemons.

When cool add the yeast and cover with a cloth, allowing it to stand overnight.

The traditional vessel for brewing was the pancheon, see damson wine.

Pour into a cask and slightly bung it down for six weeks.

Add one bottle of brandy and allow to settle.

Bottle the clear liquid without disturbing the sediment, cork and store.

This was a very popular wine in the nineteenth century, like spiced mead it is an excellent winter drink.

Alcoholic drinks were very commonly drunk with virtually every meal, they were more pleasant and probably safer than drinking water or even milk. Farmers would provide beer for their labourers and even children would be given beer (probably small beer: an early form of alco-pop?)

Chapter 6

FISH

Fish were an important food in medieval times, especially on Fridays when eating meat was banned. They were so important that many communities went to the enormous effort of digging out ponds so that they could carry out a primitive form of fish farming. The ponds were not only a source of fish but would also have provided rushes for laying on the floor or thatching and possibly as a source of birds such as swans and geese for food. It could have even been used as a washing place.

Fishing on the Nene at Woodford, 1905

The easiest way to catch the fish was with a net, which was definitely easier than angling with a rod and line. This sport was not introduced into England until 1496 when Wynkyn de Worde produced his book called *Treasyse of Fysshynge With an Angle*, though the method of angling in those days was even more inefficient than it is today – their fishing rods had a short line of plaited horse hair fixed at one end, so they could not reel in the fish. In his diary of 1672 Thomas Isham describes how he caught fish with the help of a local lad who chased the fishes from the reeds while Thomas netted them.

Until the development of the railway it was not easy to transport fresh sea fish any great distance inland but by the end of the nineteenth century this had changed and sea fish were regularly brought to Northampton, from where they would be sold or taken around the villages on a hand cart. Sea fish became very popular as did other creatures from the sea, it seems that Lord Spencer had fresh oysters delivered once a week. Sea fish were eaten in Northamptonshire as long ago as the Saxon times, but these must have been preserved in some way, possibly salted.

Once fresh sea fish became available, gradually river fish were dropped from the diets of most people.

Here is a chart briefly describing the eating qualities of a few of the more common freshwater fish.

Type of fish	Eating quality
BARBEL	These are not usually eaten in England.
BLEAK	Good to eat but rather small.
BREAM	Not good to eat.
CARP	Good to eat.
CHUBB	Good taste but bony.
DACE	Not good to eat.
GUDGEON	Good to eat.
LAMPREY	Excellent. Cook as for eels but take care to remove the two poisonous chords that run along its body before cooking.
LOACH	Delicate flavour, good to eat.
PERCH	Delicate flavour, excellent to eat.
PIKE	Excellent flesh with a good flavour.
ROACH	Good taste but bony.
RUDD	Good taste but bony.
TENCH	Good flavour but rather small.

FISH CAKES

INGREDIENTS:
> **1 lb (450g) any cooked fish**
> **with the bones and skin removed**
> **1 lb (450g) boiled potatoes**
> **1 egg**
> **6 oz (170g) breadcrumbs**

METHOD: Pound the fish in a mortar until it is a fine paste, then add the boiled potatoes and continue pounding until the paste is completely free of lumps.

Shape the paste into flat cakes which are then brushed with beaten egg, rolled in breadcrumbs and deep fried until golden brown.

This recipe from around 1865 shows that fish cakes were not invented for the benefit of automated food production though they have proved to be ideally suited to it. They were in fact a rather time-consuming way of preparing fish. Fish cakes or round fish balls were made and were considered an excellent food for breakfast.

Hobill's Mill, River Ise, Wellingborough, 1908

FRIED EELS

(Serves 4)

This recipe is taken from the *Pytchley Book of Refined Cookery and Bills of Fare* written by Major L. and published in 1886.

INGREDIENTS:
Two 1 lb (450g) eels
2 oz (55g) flour
1 egg beaten
6 oz (170g) breadcrumbs
Lard for deep frying

METHOD: Remove the skin and take out the backbone from two eels weighing a pound apiece.

Wash and carefully dry the fish then cut them into pieces about 2 inches (5cm) long.

Dust the pieces with flour, brush with beaten egg and coat with breadcrumbs before frying in hot lard for five minutes. (Major L. suggests five minutes but this is very quick and probably after cooking they would be placed in front of the fire to keep warm and crisp while the fat was draining from them, during which time they would continue cooking. It is important to make sure the eels are cooked thoroughly right to the centre.)

Serve hot with tartar sauce.

FRIED FILLET OF PERCH (OR TROUT)

Scrape off the scales from the perch, split it down the middle and remove the bones. Then dust with flour, cover with beaten egg and roll in breadcrumbs before frying as for eel in the previous recipe. After removing the fish from the fryer add some parsley to the fat and fry this for 1 minute. Hang the fried parsley in front of the fire to drain the fat from it then use it to garnish the fish.

OYSTERS AND BACON

This recipe is another from *The Pytchley Book of Refined Cookery and Bills of Fare* which was dedicated to the Countess Spencer by its author, Major L.

INGREDIENTS: **3 dozen (36) oysters**
36 very thin rashers of streaky bacon
Lard to fry
Savoury salt

METHOD: Open the oysters and remove their beards.

Wrap a slice of bacon around each oyster and secure with a small wooden skewer.

Deep fry for one minute only then dry on a sieve and serve hot. (Major L. says one minute but it is normal to fry these for at least five minutes until they are just crisp.)

Serve hot on slices of toast.

Easton Neston, Towcester

SCALLOPED OYSTERS

INGREDIENTS:

36 oysters
3 oz (85g) butter for frying and more to garnish
Savoury salt
1 lemon
3 oz (85g) breadcrumbs

METHOD: Open the oysters and remove the beards.

Save the liquid that comes from the oysters in a saucepan then simmer them in that liquid for ten minutes. (It was common to use various juices from animals mainly as a hangover from an earlier superstitious belief that they contained some essence of the animal, rather than for any culinary reasons.)

Pour off the liquid and melt three ounces of butter in the pan.

Add a squeeze of lemon and a salt spoon of savoury salt to the butter and gently simmer the oysters for a further ten minutes.

While they are cooking butter six scallop shells.

By now the oysters should be set, place six in each scallop shell and dust them with breadcrumbs.

Put a small knob of butter on top and bake at 375°F/190°C (Gas Mark 5) for five to ten minutes.

Band of Hope procession, Rushden, 1907

Chapter 7

FRUITS

This section looks at some of our traditional fruits and how they were used.

A great many fruits grow well in Northamptonshire – currants, strawberries, cherries, raspberries, apricots, apples, pears, damsons and many more were commonly grown in the county. The big houses would have fruit gardens with a good variety of fruits growing in them, farmers would have orchards where they grew a surplus of fruits for sale and the poorer people with just a small piece of land would usually manage to have a tree such as an apple, and a few fruit bushes. Because when fruits are in season there is a glut of them, even those who did not grow their own would have cheap access to a variety of fruits through friends or markets.

The following recipes largely represent methods used to preserve fruits.

Wellingborough Market Place

Apples

APPLE SAUCE

Here is a nineteenth century recipe for that traditional accompaniment to pork, apple sauce.

INGREDIENTS:

1 lb (450g) cooking apples
½ oz (15g) butter
1 fl oz (30ml) water
1 fl oz (30ml) lemon juice
2 good pinches of cinnamon or grated nutmeg
Sugar to taste.

METHOD: Peel and core the apples, place them and all the other ingredients except the sugar in a saucepan and warm very gently.

As the apples soften, the heat can be increased very slightly.

Continue gently heating until the apple is soft and pulpy (15 to 20 minutes depending on the apples).

Beat the apple to a frothy pulp then return to the heat and add the sugar to taste.

When all the sugar has dissolved stop heating and serve hot or cold as a tasty accompaniment for pork, goose or duck.

Apples are one of the few fruits that can be stored without special treatment, they can be eaten fresh or cooked in a variety of ways to make pies, jams, chutney and a whole lot more. It is hardly surprising that such a versatile and easily grown fruit was very popular and that they have already been mentioned in other sections, see Finedon apples, apple chutney and apple pie.

In the time of Elizabeth I, apples were commonly used in stews and it is rather fun to judiciously add them to casseroles especially with pork and they also go well in home-made pork sausages.

In the nineteenth century apples were preserved as *apple cheese* which is just another name for apple jam, see damson cheese in this section.

CRAB JELLY

This clear, beautifully flavoured jam is an ideal way for using crab apples or those tiny summer windfalls which, though unripe and sour at the start, turn into this excellent jelly. The recipe below from *The Midland Counties Cookery Book* (c1900) was submitted by Mrs Hemmings of Northampton.

INGREDIENTS:
5 lb (2.25kg) crab apples
5 pints (2.8 litres) water
Approximately 6 lb (2.7kg) sugar
Lemons, juice to taste

METHOD: Put the water and whole apples together in a preserving pan and boil until the apples turn to pulp.

Strain the liquid through muslin overnight. Do not squeeze to get extra juice as this will make the jelly cloudy.

Add lemon juice as required.

Measure the volume of the juice obtained and for each pint add 1 lb of sugar (for each litre add 750g of sugar).

Place all the ingredients in a preserving pan and in the time honoured way boil it until it sets.

Sterilise the bottles and their lids using boiling water, leave them to drain and while still hot stand them on a wooden board and pour in the hot jam. This is to prevent the jars cracking because of uneven heating.

Lifeboat fundraising in Northampton, Whitsuntide, 20 May 1907

Apricots

"TO PRESERVE APRICOCKES"

This recipe for bottled apricots comes from the Kirby Hall Receipts.

INGREDIENTS: **2 lb (900g) stoned and skinned apricots**
2 lb (900g) sugar
1 pint (570ml) water

METHOD: Cover the stoned, skinned apricots with 1 pint (570ml) of water and 1 lb (450g) of sugar and leave to stand overnight.

Next day warm the mixture until it boils then add the rest of the sugar and keep on warming until it has all dissolved.

Place the hot fruit into Kilner jars that have been scalded with boiling water. (If the hot jars are placed on a towel or a wooden board they are less likely to crack.) Pour the hot syrup over the fruit and seal the jars immediately.

Aynho Park

Of all the villages in Northamptonshire, Aynho, the most south-westerly, is also the one most closely associated with the apricot. It has been grown there probably since Tudor times and it was once the custom for villagers to pay part of their rent to the Lord of the Manor in apricots. They are suited to our well drained soils but need protection such as in a greenhouse, though they can be grown in the open against a south or south-east facing wall where they will normally produce fruit in August and September.

Apricots are not the best fruit to eat uncooked but they preserve well. The easiest way to do this is to dry them and in this state they will last a full year or more. Before use, dried apricots have to be soaked in water for at least three hours until they become soft, they can then be pureed and cooked in a variety of ways. If you should feel the urge to dry your own apricots it is done by cutting them in half and leaving them in a warm place at about 130°F/55°C. An airing-cupboard is fine even if it is a little cooler than this, however it is important they do not get above 140°F/60°C.

Apricots make an excellent jam using equal weights of sugar and stoned fruit. Some people like to add the broken kernels to the jam as it cooks, and this does add a slightly nutty taste to the preserve.

Blackberries

It is still easy to find blackberries, in hedgerows and on the margins of woods. How much easier it must have been when there were both more hedges and more woods. There are various ways that they can be used as food and they have a good flavour eaten fresh with sugar and cream though it is important they are well soaked to remove any unwanted insects. Blackberry jam (bramble jelly), blackberry tart, and bramble wine are all good though the real classic is blackberry and apple pie. There are other, perhaps less familiar uses of the bramble, such as dyes for cloth. The blackberry on its own gives a violet colour to the cloth but when boiled with ivy leaves it becomes a black dye.

An interesting thing to try is collecting young bramble leaves in spring or summer and leave them to dry. These can then be used with boiling water in the time honoured way to make a tea which is drunk without milk.

The last unusual way of using blackberries is to boil them with parsnips. Boiled blackberries have a beautiful flavour but they do need sugar to make them palatable. The poor were not always able to afford sugar, especially at the time of the American

War of Independence, America was an important supplier of sugar and the price rose rapidly when we could no longer get it from them. The solution was to boil the blackberries with parsnips so that the sweetness from the root vegetable would make the blackberries edible. Does this have a hint of desperation about it?

High Street, Pytchley

Cherries

TO PRESERVE CHERRIES IN BRANDY

INGREDIENTS:
6 lb (2.7kg) cherries (Maraschino cherries)
1½ lb (680g) sugar
1½ pints (850ml) brandy

METHOD: Divide the ingredients proportionally between several wide necked bottles. Insert corks into the necks and make sure they are sealed before leaving for at least three months.

The cherry orchards of seventeenth century Northampton have already been mentioned (see Chapter 3, Lamport Hall). There are two different types of cherry, the culinary cherry which has a sour taste and is not suitable for eating raw, and the sweet dessert cherry. The morello is probably the best known culinary cherry and it is a common practice to grow these among the dessert cherries to pollinate them (many dessert cherries are self infertile). Cherry trees are not indigenous to this country having been brought over by the Romans, but they grow well in places where the soil is well drained, as in Northamptonshire.

Cherries are used in various ways such as in pies or cakes and cherry jam is very pleasant. Attempts were made to store cherries by drying them in much the same way as apricots and Finedon apples, but they had virtually no commercial success. Storing them in brandy as described above was altogether more satisfactory.

The Drapery, Northampton

Currants

CURRANT WINE

For wine making it is the red and white currants that are preferred over the more bitter blackcurrant. They are best picked in bunches from which the fruits can be removed using a fork to pull the currants from the stalks, and if a few small bits of stalk remain it will not affect the wine. The recipe below comes from the early years of the nineteenth century (c1817).

INGREDIENTS:
7 lb (3.15kg) currants (red and/or white)
5-6 pints (about 3 litres) water
3 lb (1.35kg) sugar
Yeast

METHOD: Squeeze the currants in your hands and collect the juice.

Strain the juice through a hair sieve then make it up to eight pints using fresh spring water (I get my fresh spring water from a tap in the kitchen).

Put it in a cask with the sugar. (The recipe does not say to add yeast because that fungus had yet to be discovered in 1817, but as it is unwise to rely on natural fermentation a little wine yeast should be added.)

Keep filling it up every day as long as it works. When it has finished stop it up and close. (It would be better to decant the liquid from the sediment, stopper it in a separate container and leave it in a cool place to clear before bottling.)

South Bridge, Northampton, after widening in 1914

All three types of currants, black, red and white were popular in fruit gardens because the bushes are prolific and they do not take up a lot of space. It is the blackcurrant which is most widely used in cooked products such as blackcurrant jam, blackcurrant jelly, pies, and tarts and it also finds its way into certain vitamin-rich cordial drinks. They may be highly prized as a source of iron and Vitamins B and C but anyone who has spent hours 'topping and tailing 'em' (removing the stalks and scaly flower remnants) might be forgiven for having mixed feelings about them. Topping and tailing was a job for the family out in the garden in their oldest clothes so the blackcurrant stains did not matter, a time consuming occupation that is perhaps not compatible with modern living.

Redcurrant jelly is a traditional accompaniment to game but it is also good served with mutton or pork. Indeed a little added to casseroles, but only enough for the extra sweetness to be barely perceptible, makes a good casserole even more tasty.

Hobill's Mill, Wellingborough, 1903

Damsons

DAMSON CHEESE

INGREDIENTS: **3 lb (1.35kg) fully ripe damsons**
6-8 oz (about 200g) sugar
6 oz (170g) isinglass

METHOD: Remove the stones and pulp the fruit.

Put the pulp in an oven-proof dish with the sugar and place in an oven at 325°F/160°C (Gas Mark 3) for about 45 minutes.

Strain through a fine sieve into a saucepan and stirring all the time add the isinglass.

Boil until it sets (testing as for jam).

Dispense into warmed jars as for jam.

Damsons are like dark bitter plums with a green flesh, they have a good full flavour which is useful in tarts and jams but they also make very good wine which has already been described in the section on drinks. Like plums, damsons grow best in well drained soil but they prefer slightly wetter conditions than the plum and grow well in Northamptonshire.

Damson cheese is the old English name for Damson jam though according to Mrs E. Whitehead's recipe book (c1850) it was made using isinglass. Isinglass comes from the dried bladders of fish of which the best source was believed to be the Russian sturgeon. Dissolved in water it behaves much like gelatine and was once widely used to make blancmanges and jellies.

PICKLED DAMSONS

INGREDIENTS:

1 lb (450g) Damsons
5 fl oz (140ml) white vinegar
2 cloves
1 cinnamon stick
2 good pinches of red pepper
1 lb (450g) sugar.

METHOD: Wash the damsons carefully and put them in a preserving jar.

Fill the jar with boiling water being careful to scald the rim all the way round.

Also scald the lid thoroughly and leave it loosely on top of the jar.

Put the vinegar, sugar and spices in a saucepan and bring to the boil.

Tip the water away from the damsons and replace it with the boiling vinegar.

Add more cold vinegar to cover the fruit.

Put the lid on and tighten when cool.

The old cottages, Abington, Northampton

Gooseberries

GOOSEBERRY CREAM

In the nineteenth century, fruit creams were very popular. They consisted of fruit juice made by squeezing the real fruits, which was then thickened with cream and solidified in a mould with gelatine or isinglass so it looked rather like a modern blancmange. The recipe below is from the Finch-Hatton household.

INGREDIENTS:

1 lb (450g) gooseberries
½ pint (280ml) double cream
3 oz (85g) sugar
¾ oz (21g) gelatine
3 tablespoons water

METHOD: Scald the gooseberries with boiling water, thoroughly drain off all the water and mash them to a pulp.

Strain the pulp through a cloth.

Dissolve the gelatine in three tablespoons of hot water.

Add the sugar to the gelatine and continue warming very gently until the sugar dissolves. (A good way to do this is to place the container in a saucepan of boiling water to avoid burning the gelatine.)

Beat the cream until it is stiff.

Pour the warm fruit juice into the gelatine then add it to the cream.

Stir lightly but thoroughly to mix then pour into a one pint mould.

Leave in a cool place to set.

Gooseberries were introduced into England in medieval times and became a very popular food in those days. At Whitsun the traditional food was a gooseberry pie made with a filling of chicken, gooseberries, eggs and butter.

Figs

Palm Sunday was known as Fig Sunday and it was the custom for both rich and poor in Milton Malsor to eat figs on that day.

Abington Park, Northampton, 1914

Figs are grown in Northamptonshire in the open and anyone wishing to try it should use a hardy variety such as 'Brown Turkey' or 'Brunswick'. Unfortunately without growing them under glass they would not be edible at Easter.

Pears

BAKED WARDENS

Pear trees are slow growing and the countryman's saying is 'Plant pears for your heirs' The monks at Warden Abbey just over the border in Bedfordshire developed the pears which became known as Wardens. Warden pies were popular even in Shakespeare's time, the pastry being filled with pears, prunes and raisins and spiced with mace, ginger and nutmeg. It was a pie for cold winter days.

Baked Warden pears were sold at local fairs. This was one of those foods that people always seemed to mention when talking of the old fairs, later it would be brandy snaps or toffee-apples and, more recently, candy-floss.

Pitsford, 1911

BAKED PEARS

INGREDIENTS:

4 large firm pears
¼ pint (140ml) red wine
¼ pint (140ml) water
1 oz (30g) brown sugar
A good pinch of cinnamon
A good pinch of ground ginger

METHOD: Peel and core the pears.

Place them in an oven proof dish together with the other ingredients. The pears should be covered by the liquid.

Bake in a preheated oven at 350°F/180°C – Gas Mark 4 – for 30 minutes, until the pears are soft.

In the very heart of Northamptonshire (as it is now without the Soke of Peterborough) at its geographical centre – Pitsford – there was once a baker who in the autumn baked pears to give to the children of the village. If the recipe above is prepared using tinned pears the syrup from the tin can be mixed with spiced cider to make a drink rather like the Cattern Bowl. It is a perfect accompaniment for these rather spicy, very delicious pears and a great favourite of yours truly.

Pitsford Hall

Quinces

QUINCE JELLY

Various fruits could be used to make this jelly. Hard fruits such as apples and pears need to be boiled first but soft fruits such as cherries and raspberries could be used without boiling. This is based on a submission by Mrs Rooke in *A Northamptonshire Recipe Book* (c1900).

INGREDIENTS:

3 lb (1.35kg) quinces, weighed after the fruit has been peeled and cored
1½ pints (850ml) water
1¼ oz (35g) tartaric acid
2¼ lb (1kg) sugar

1 oz (30g) gelatine
1 pint (570ml) syrup
1 pint (570ml) water

METHOD: *The syrup*:

Put the peeled and cored quinces in a saucepan with the water and boil until soft.

Add the tartaric acid, replace the lid and leave to stand for 24 hours.

Strain the liquid into a clean container and add the sugar. Stir occasionally with very gentle warming until all the sugar has dissolved.

The jelly:

Soak the gelatine in a little of the water as directed on the packet.

Boil the rest of the water and add the gelatine stirring all the time to dissolve it.

Allow it to cool for a few minutes then add the syrup made previously.

Stir until evenly distributed and pour into moulds.

It is a great pity that quinces are not generally available as they were once very popular and are really useful in cooking. If you want them the best way is to grow them yourself and fortunately this is fairly easy.

Although quinces cannot be eaten raw they are useful either mixed with other fruits or on their own in jams and jellies, tarts or pies. They can also be added to cider and apparently they greatly improve its taste and quality. Quinces have a mucilaginous thickening property which made them highly prized from the time they were introduced by the Romans until the reign of Queen Victoria, but since then they have lost popularity, possibly for no better reason than that their knobbly appearance is not sufficiently attractive on the fruiterers' shelves. Perhaps fruits, like people, should be judged by their qualities rather than by their appearance.

Great Oakley

Raspberries

AN EXCELLENT RECEIPT FOR BOTTLING FRUIT

The recipe given below comes from the 1860s and needs to be followed very thoroughly if it is to be successful.

INGREDIENTS: **9 lb (4kg) red and/or white currants**
5 lb (2.25kg) sugar
sufficient water to barely cover the fruit

METHOD: Place all the ingredients in a large saucepan or preserving pan and heat to boiling.

Simmer for ten minutes with very gentle stirring so as not to bruise the fruits.

Pour the hot mixture into an earthenware pot which has previously been scalded with boiling water. Immediately replace the lid and leave several hours to cool.

When cold pour into wide necked bottles that have been thoroughly scalded with boiling water.

Cover with a bladder which has also been scalded and seal thoroughly.

This is an attempt to preserve the fruit in a natural state. It can be used not only for raspberries but many other fruits such as red and white currants, strawberries, pears and plums. It is specially attractive when a variety of fruits are packed in layers. It is important that the bottles and fruit are properly sterilized and the seal remains unbroken. If this is done they will stay edible for long periods – easily over a year.

RASPBERRY VINEGAR

This recipe is from Mrs E. Whitehead (c1850) it makes an interesting present and could hardly be simpler.

INGREDIENTS: **1 lb (450g) raspberries**
                         2 pints (1.1 litres) white wine vinegar.

METHOD: Only use the good undamaged berries. Wash them gently, place them in an attractively shaped bottle and cover with a good quality white wine vinegar.

Grafton Underwood

Strawberries

STRAWBERRY JELLY

INGREDIENTS:

The fruit
1 lb (450g) of good quality fresh strawberries
8 oz (225g) sugar
¾ pint (420ml) brandy

The jelly
4 lb (1.8kg) sugar
1 ½ oz (42g) gelatine
2 lemons
7 fl oz (200ml) sherry or Madeira

METHOD: *The fruit:*

Wash the fruit and remove the green sepals.

Place in a bowl and sprinkle on the sugar.

Pour the brandy over them and leave to soak for at least three hours.

The jelly:

Put the gelatine to soak in a little water at the same time as soaking the strawberries in brandy.

Squeeze the juice from two lemons and strain to remove any solid bits.

Put about a quarter of the water in a saucepan to boil. Then remove it from the heat, add the soaked gelatine and stir until it has dissolved.

Add the sugar, the lemon juice and the remainder of the water and warm gently stirring all the time until the sugar has dissolved.

Add the sherry and pour into a bowl.

When it has nearly cooled but is still liquid, remove the strawberries from the brandy and place them in the jelly. (Or do it in two layers.)

This recipe comes from *The Pytchley Book of Refined Cookery and Bills of Fare.*

Tomatoes

TOMATO JELLY

The recipe below is for clear tomato jam (c1865).

INGREDIENTS:
**2 lb (900g) tomatoes
2 lb (900g) apples
2 lemons
2 cloves
½ nutmeg grated
4 lb (1.8kg) sugar**

METHOD: Peel and core the apples then cut the flesh into small pieces.

Chop the tomatoes into a saucepan so that none of the liquid is lost

Remove the rind of the lemons and grate it into the saucepan.

Add the cloves and grated nutmeg to the saucepan and heat gently until the apple becomes a pulp. It may be necessary to add just a couple of tablespoons of water to stop the apple sticking to the bottom of the pan.

When it has become a pulp, strain through a fine sieve.

Add the sugar and boil until it gels.

Put into warmed jars in the usual way.

At the time of this recipe tomatoes were not widely used. Some people even thought they were poisonous. We who are more familiar with them in casseroles, pizza toppings or salads might find this use of tomatoes a refreshing idea.

Chapter 8

THE FOOD OF THE POOR

The records from the big houses find their way into historic archives and these are good sources of such recipes. However, it is not so easy to find material about the poor, so clues have to be found elsewhere. Sources such as autobiographies sometimes give an insight into the lives of the poor – for example, the *Recollections of William Arnold*. There are records of cookery courses run for the poor women in Victorian Northamptonshire and there is also a rather remarkable newspaper article from the *Northamptonshire Mercury* of 8 November 1757. In that year the wheat harvest failed resulting in a considerable rise in the cost of flour and much hardship especially for the poor.

Meadow Lane, Isham

Dr James Stonehouse of Northampton published several recipes in an article in the *Northamptonshire Mercury*. In those days the rich were taught that their affluence was a gift from God and it was their duty to help the poor. Dr Stonehouse made a plea for the rich to provide food for the poor and the following recipes are his suggestion of how it could be done. His recipe for 'Beer made with Treacle' has already been given but he made other suggestions such as baking bread using half the normal flour and making up the other half with mashed potato. Nearly two hundred years later similar recipes were published by the government during World War II.

Two more of Dr Stonehouse's recipes follow.

Dr Stonehouse's Recipes

BURGOUT (BURGOO)

Dr Stonehouse claimed that the recipe given below was sufficient for a family of six, in his words it was *'Design'd for fuch Families as are very neceffitous.'*

INGREDIENTS: **2 pints (560ml) oatmeal**
4 pints (1.1 litres) water
Salt and butter according to availability

METHOD: Put the oatmeal in a large saucepan and add the water little by little, with brisk stirring.

Keep simmering for 15 minutes, stirring all the while.

Before serving add a little salt and butter if available.

From the nutritional viewpoint this is not a balanced diet but it does provide energy and so would probably satisfy the most pressing needs of a working family. Dr James was giving good advice.

'As thick as burgoo' Apparently a local saying recorded in *Baker's Northamptonshire Glossary* (1845).

VEGETABLE STEW

(6 people for a day)

The next recipe is another from Dr Stonehouse and is much closer to a balanced meal than Burgout.

INGREDIENTS:

2 lb (900g) meat – beef, pork or mutton
4 oz (115g) carrots
8 oz (225g) turnips
Cabbage or other greens as available
2 lb (900g) potatoes
2-3 onions
1½ lb (680g) of oatmeal
Pepper and salt to taste
16 pints (9 litres) of water

METHOD: Cut the meat into very small pieces, place it in the water and simmer for three hours.

Add the sliced carrots, finely diced turnips, sliced cabbage or greens, sliced onion and chopped potatoes to the mixture.

Thicken by adding the oatmeal and keep simmering for another hour until the vegetables are soft.

Add salt and pepper to taste and keep warm.

Serve throughout the day.

This is actually a tasty meal and one that is very nourishing. The good doctor's suggestions were sensible.

Mrs Dale's Recipes

In late Victorian times the Northamptonshire Council started running cookery classes to teach poor women how to cook cheap nutritious meals. The school was established by Mary K. Dale who in 1891 published a book called *Popular Recipes* which contained many of the recipes from the course, two of which were pearl barley soup and baked rice pudding.

PEARL BARLEY SOUP

(Serves 12)

INGREDIENTS:
1 lb (450g) pearl barley
3 lb (1.35kg) mutton bones
2 leeks
Half a turnip
Pepper and salt to taste
6 pints (3.4 litres) water

METHOD: Shred the vegetables very fine.

Wash the pearl barley.

Wash the bones.

Place everything together with the water in the saucepan and bring to the boil.

After five minutes skim off the scum.

Continue boiling for three hours, with frequent stirring.

Remove the bones and add salt and pepper to taste.

Even after the husks have been removed from the barley seeds, they have a brown skin on them. This can be removed mechanically and what is left is pearlized barley (pearl barley) which is often used to thicken broth such as Scotch broth or mutton broth as well as in Mrs Dale's Pearl Barley Soup.

BAKED RICE PUDDING

Rice pudding is filling, cheap and has been used as a dessert for centuries. The recipe below was intended for poor families and came from *Practical Cookery* (1891) written by Mary K. Dale of the Northamptonshire School of Cookery.

INGREDIENTS:

4 oz (115g) pudding rice
2 oz (55g) sugar
1 pint (570ml) milk
1 oz (30g) shredded suet
pinch of grated nutmeg (optional)

METHOD: Put a saucepan of water on the cooker to boil.

While it is heating wash the rice.

Sprinkle the rice into the boiling water and simmer it for five minutes.

Spread about half the suet over the bottom of the pie dish. If you prefer just smear a little butter round the inside of the pie dish.

Add the rice and sugar.

Pour in the milk

Sprinkle the remainder of the suet over the top. (Or float a few small pieces of butter on the surface).

Put a light dusting of grated nutmeg over the surface if preferred.

Put in a preheated oven at 325°F/160°C (Gas Mark 3) for one and a half to two hours.

(Stir once or twice when the rice is beginning to cook to stop it sticking.)

There were several ways of dressing up rice pudding, adding raisins was popular, or when the pudding was nearly cooked one could press some tinned peaches into the rice and cover with meringue, then replace it in the oven. Not that Mary Dale would have approved of such extravagances for her poor people.

Chapter 9

COOKERY BOOKS

Up to the nineteenth century few cookery books had been published and each cook had only hand written records for reference. During the nineteenth century there were several recipe books produced of which *Mrs Beeton's book of Household Management* is probably the best known. Towards the end of the nineteenth century there were several local books published one of which was *The Pytchley Book of Refined Cookery and Bills of Fare* by Major L. (A not very cryptic nom-de-plume for Major Landon) published in 1886 by Chapman and Hall. Another was *Practical Cookery* (1891) written by Mary K. Dale of the Northamptonshire School of Cookery, which featured recipes for the poor.

Great Brington

In the first decade of the twentieth century there were at least three compilation books made up of recipes sent in by Northamptonshire women. These are interesting as an indication of the dishes those ladies liked, for example Ginger Cake was very commonly mentioned. Other similar compilation books have been produced, mainly as fund raising exercises for particular groups, but these, with the exception of one, have been ignored here as being too recent for consideration as 'traditional' cooking. The exception is the *Northamptonshire Federation of Women's Institutes' Recipe Book* of which several editions have been printed. From it one learns how to be economical when ironing with gas, that old enamelled baths may be cleaned easily using a rag dampened with paraffin (not a good idea to try this with modern baths) and many other fascinating titbits. The recipes for Northamptonshire Cheese Cakes, Brigstock Pickle and A Good Northamptonshire Pudding (all in Chapter 11) were taken from this book.

Isham

Major L.

The Pytchley book of Refined Cookery and Bills of Fare by Major L. What a frustrating but fascinating book this is. Many of the recipes are outrageously lavish, often meat is cooked in one extremely complex and costly sauce only to have it tipped away and replaced with another even more costly sauce to garnish the meat for serving. The book is written in an autocratic, individualistic manner by a man who (one suspects) never cooked any of the recipes himself but relied on the information given him by his cook, and yet in it are some very good and interesting recipes of which the following are a few.

CROÛTES

For this recipe some crispy rolls are cut in half and the soft centres removed and crumbed. Crisp the hollowed crusts in an oven and fill with chopped chicken and ham (Major L. also suggests using sheep's brains flavoured with cream but in these days of BSE it is probably wisest to avoid eating nervous systems). Fry the breadcrumbs and cover the croûtes with them, return to the oven and serve hot.

BEEFSTEAK PIE

Cut about two pounds of fillet of beef into thin slices, and also slice three or four kidneys, slice also half a dozen hard-boiled eggs. Arrange in a pie-dish in alternate rows, pepper and salting and sprinkling with chopped parsley and chives each row of meat until the dish is full; pour over it some consommé (No. 1); lay a border round the top of the dish of Pastry (No. 366), and having wetted it, cover with a covering of same paste; egg the surface and make a hole in the centre; bake for one hour or more in a moderately-heated oven, and pour some Espagnole Sauce (No. 34) over it.

PLUM PUDDING

(Six large helpings)

INGREDIENTS: *The pudding*

4 oz (115g) plain flour
4 oz (115g) bread crumbs
5 oz (140g) sugar
A little salt
8 oz (225g) shredded suet
8 oz (225g) stoned raisins
4 oz (115g) currants
4 oz (115g) minced apple
4 oz (115g) candied peel
4 eggs

The sauce

4 oz (115g) butter
4 oz (115g) icing sugar
4 tablespoons of brandy
2 tablespoons sherry

METHOD: *The pudding:*

Clean and stalk the currants.

Mix the flour, bread crumbs, sugar, salt and suet together thoroughly.

Mix in the fruit and chopped candied peel.

Beat the eggs and add them to the mixture, stirring thoroughly.

Smear the inside of the pudding cloth with butter.

Place the mixture in the cloth and tie it up.

Put a trivet in the bottom of a saucepan of water and place the pudding on this.

Leave in just-boiling water for up to six hours.

The sauce:

Mix the butter and sugar to a paste.

Add the brandy and sherry beating vigorously to a cream.

In Victorian times, before harvests had been automated, they went on for weeks and every one who could would help. Bringing in the last load was a time for celebration and they would sing:

> *'Harvest Home! Pays and Brun!*
> *Three plum puddings are better nor none!'*

Plum pudding is what today we would recognise as Christmas pudding. It is a good old pudding dating back at least to the eleventh century. Plum pudding originally did have plums in it and in *Baker's Northamptonshire Glossary* (1845) there is a record of the terms 'whispering pudding' and 'hooting pudding'. In the whispering plum pudding, the plums were close together, whereas in the hooting one they were few and far between. The recipe for plum pudding given by Major L. was more like our Christmas pudding with no plums in it (a silent pudding?). This is a very good recipe and well worth cooking.

Polebrook, near Oundle

TO HANG VENISON

Hang a haunch of fat venison as long as it can be hung without being high. Fresh venison is hard, stale venison is simply a disappointment and annoyance to everyone in the house; it reminds one of kennel soup, and a more disgusting aroma than that it is difficult to find. I have been reminded, however, frequently of this poisonous effluvia. To prevent this I would beg my readers to flour their haunches of venison and wipe daily, and dust with pepper, which annoys flies very much. As soon as it begins to smell dress it at once. If properly taken care of in a good larder, it should hang a fortnight in the summer and a month in the autumn, unless the weather is very bad.

You may not need to hang venison, but if you ever have a dozen larks or fieldfares to cook in a pie just consult the good major's Recipe No. 383 – Small Bird Pie.

The Pytchley Book of Refined Cookery and Bills of Fare has been a useful source of recipes for this book and fascinating to read, reflecting as it does the attitudes of a Victorian huntsman.

Lizzie Cox

Doing the research for this book was at times profoundly moving. When handling an actual recipe that had been painstakingly neatly written out perhaps several hundred years earlier one cannot help thinking and wondering about its writer, and when in with the recipes so carefully saved is a letter from the cook's lover how could anyone not be moved. Out of all these moments one especially stands out for me. Unlike the other books in this section it was handwritten in a school book. The writer was Lizzie Cox and she was in 1888 just ten years old. It seems that there were ten Saturday morning lessons held in the School playground along Kettering Road, Northampton, and each lesson consisted of several demonstrations and one practical. There were a lot of basic, cheap recipes all written up very carefully by Lizzie who so faithfully recorded even the tutor's rather Victorian attitudes to cooking. Dearest Lizzie – I hope you had a good life.

Food is cooked that it may be made acceptable to the taste and digestible. The chief art of cooking is not to let any of the good things that each food contains get out and be wasted during cooking, also to make the food tender and easy of digestion. The different ways of cooking are Roasting, Broiling, Boiling, Baking, Stewing and Frying of which boiling is the most economical.

ROASTING. This is cooking meat by suspending it before a clear fire, and keeping it turned round. A bottle-jack or a piece of twisted worsted is used to suspend it. Two things are necessary for nice roasting, a clear bright fire and frequent basting. You must place your meat close to a good fire at first to harden the outside albumen, to form a coat or skin to keep in the juices, this will take about half an hour. Then draw the joint back and allow it to cook more slowly.

Question	*What is albumen?*
Answer	*Albumen is a sticky substance resembling the white of an egg.*
Question	*What does albumen do in the body and where is it found*
Answer	*Albumen is the flesh form and it is found in the white of an egg, in lean, in bread, in fish, in milk.*
Question	*How is albumen hardened?*
Answer	*Albumen is hardened by heat.*

TIME. Quarter of an hour to each pound and 20 minutes over. When the joint is done, little jets of steam will come hissing from the inside, then dredge the joint lightly with flour, nicely brown. Strain the dripping out of the pan, drench with boiling water, add a little pepper and salt, put the joint on a hot dish and strain the gravy over the top.

FRYING. Meat cooked in a frying pan is a wasteful way of cooking and means poverty to many a poor home, it is often used for quickness, to cook steaks and chops which are made hard and indigestible, when half the quantity of meat would make a good dinner with vegetables when gently stewed in a little water, and much less trouble in the end, besides being a thoroughly nutritious and tender dish. The frying pan may be used to advantage to warm up cold vegetables, cold puddings, and to fry liver and bacon, etc. Bacon is much nicer toasted than fried.

GROUND RICE PIES

INGREDIENTS:

The filling
Rind of half a lemon
1 pint (570ml) milk
3 oz (85g) ground rice
3 oz (85g) sugar
3 oz (85g) sultanas
Ground nutmeg

The pastry
8 oz (225g) flour
1 teaspoon baking powder
A pinch of salt
2 oz (55g) lard
1 oz (30g) butter
Water

Geddington Band, Coronation 1911

METHOD: To make the filling put the milk and lemon rind together in a saucepan and boil.

Remove the lemon rind then stir in the ground rice until it thickens.

Add the sugar and sultanas and stir with gentle heat for five minutes.

To make the pastry put the flour, baking powder and salt into a mixing bowl.

Rub in the butter until there are no lumps then mix in sufficient flour to make a firm pastry.

Lay the pastry on a floured board and roll to ½ inch (12mm) thick.

Spread with half the lard and dredge lightly with flour.

Fold in half so the lard and flour are in the centre and roll out again.

Spread with lard and flour as before.

Fold in half but this time roll until ⅓ inch (8mm) thick.

Line a pie dish with the pastry and add the ground rice mixture.

Sprinkle a good pinch of ground nutmeg on the surface and bake at 375°F/190°C (Gas Mark 5) for 30 minutes.

The Grafton Pack, Paulerspury

RABBIT PIE

Rabbit pies can be made with just rabbit meat on its own but as with game especially rook pie it seems much more common for it to be mixed with other meats such as ham or beef. Rabbit has a taste which is quite unmistakable and for the many people who were brought up with this flavour it is very evocative of their childhood. No need to dilute its flavour with more expensive meats for them.

INGREDIENTS:

1 Rabbit
8 oz (225g) steak
12 oz (340g) plain flour
3 oz (85g) lard
2 teaspoons baking powder
A pinch of salt
15 fl oz (420g) water
1 dessertspoon of salt
1 saltspoon of pepper.

METHOD: Cut the rabbit into joints.

Cut the steak into strips

Mix the flour and seasoning

Put the pieces of rabbit and steak into it.

Arrange in a pie dish.

Pour over ½ pint (280ml) of the water.

Stew in an oven at 275°F/140°C (Gas Mark 1) for 30 minutes.

While it is cooking put the flour, baking powder, and a pinch of salt into a mixing bowl.

Rub in the lard.

Add the remainder of the water to make it a firm paste.

Roll out and line a greased pie tin with the pastry.

Fill with the mixture and cover with pastry.

Cut away the surplus pastry.

Moisten the edges and seal by pressing them together.

Roll out the off cuts of pastry and cut into strips. Moisten one side of each strip and lay them over the surface in the form of a lattice.

Brush with beaten egg.

Make a hole in the centre.

Bake at 325°F/160°C (Gas Mark 4) for 1 hour.

Mr W. Bree of Northampton

BEEF PATTIES

(8 patties)

INGREDIENTS: **8 oz (225g) beef**
12 oz (340g) plain flour
1½ teaspoons of baking powder
A pinch of salt
4 oz (115ml) dripping
Salt and pepper to season
⅜ pint (210ml) water

METHOD: Put the flour, salt and baking powder into a mixing bowl.

Add the dripping and mix in by hand until it is free of lumps.

Add the water by degrees until it forms a smooth paste.

Lay on a floured board and roll out to a quarter inch thick.

Cut the pastry into 16 rounds.

Use eight of the rounds to line patty tins.

Cut the meat into small pieces.

Season with salt and pepper.

Put a tablespoon of meat in each.

Moisten the edges of the pastry and use the other eight rounds to seal the patties.

Press down the edge.

Prick the top with a fork.

Bake on a flat tin at 350°F/180°C (Gas Mark 4) for 35 minutes.

Chapter 10

FOOD AND OCCUPATIONS

Bakers

Bakers have been mentioned a lot so far. They, along with other tradesmen such as blacksmiths, were often real characters in their village, frequently turning their hands to anything that would make them a few extra pennies. They would be up early lighting the ovens and mixing the dough so by the time the other workers were on their way to work the bakers had finished the hardest part of their day. While perhaps their wives were selling the bread and cakes (cigarettes, pork pies, etc.) the bakers were free to do other things like tend the garden, grow fruit (or watercress), anything that would bring in a little extra cash.

Watercress Harry

They would even work on Sunday, roasting other people's dinners, and how they must have enjoyed selling the embers from their ovens to fill the Dicky pots of the lace makers. The Dicky pot was a metal container with holes in the sides. When filled with glowing embers and placed under the full skirts they used to wear it kept the legs warm. This was originally used by the lacemakers who did not want to sit by an open fire because the smoke would discolour their lace.

The baker would know everybody in the village. He would complain about how he had to work hard, how he had to be up early and how really he was charging so little that he was virtually losing money. The reality was that he did work hard and steadily every day but many labourers worked harder for less.

In Northampton there was a baker called A. J. Hannell who kept a recipe book over the period 1885-1890, and it shows the range of products he produced.

Halfpenny Banbury Cakes
Grantham Ginger Bread (6d per lb)
Best Spice Nuts
Best Pound Cake
Plum Cakes
Tea Cakes
Thick Gingerbread
Snap Gingerbread
Windsor Cake
Sugar Cake
Sponge Biscuits
Rock Biscuits
York Biscuits
Common Pat
Buns
Crumpets
Muffins
Pound Cake (1 shilling)
Currant Cakes (6d per lb)

In addition to the above he would also bake several types of bread.

Banbury Cakes

These traditionally spicy oval cakes made of puff pastry containing dried fruits and peel were traditionally kept warm in a flannel-lined wire basket.

Ginger Bread

This dates back to medieval times and would have been highly ornamented with painted cloves stuck in it to resemble jewels. Gilding the gingerbread was literally that, it was painted with egg white to seal it, then ornamented with gold leaf. These were given as presents but the custom was dying out in Hannell's time and the gingerbread baked was probably more like the blocks of gingerbread we know today.

Portion of supplies for Sunday School treat, Rushden, July 1916

Spice Nuts

These were what we know as ginger nuts (ginger biscuits).

Pound Cakes

These were so named because they were supposedly made with a pound each of flour, butter and sugar, mixed with ten eggs and traditionally flavoured with brandy. Hannell used 1 lb butter, 1¼ lb lump sugar, 1½ lb flour and ten eggs well beaten and strained through a sieve. These were mixed together and flavoured with essence of lemon.

Plum Cakes

These were the same mixture as for pound cakes but with 1 lb of currants and ½ oz candied peel added to the mixture.

Tea Cakes

These traditionally come from Yorkshire where they were made with yeast, flour, milk and eggs. They were baked as small round cakes which while still hot were broken in half and dipped in melted butter. The two halves were then put back together again and served hot, but it is a recipe that has been changed many times, for example Hannell's cakes just had currants sprinkled on the top.

Church tea, Kettering

BREAD

(Makes 3 large loaves)

INGREDIENTS:
3½ lb (1.6kg) good quality plain flour
1 oz (30g) yeast
1 teaspoon castor sugar
1 dessert spoon salt
1½ pints (850ml) warm water

METHOD: If you are using dry yeast follow the instructions on the packet, then make up to 1½ pints with warm water. Traditionally fresh yeast was used and if you have this rub the yeast and sugar into the water and leave to stand for about 15 minutes before using.

Sift the flour into a mixing bowl, add the salt and gradually mix in the water and fermenting yeast.

Cover the dish with a damp cloth and leave in a warm place until the 'sponge' starts to rise. This takes 20 to 30 mins.

Knead on a floured surface for 15 minutes.

Divide the dough into three.

To make a Coburg loaf roll the dough into a ball and make two deep cuts at right angles across the top.

To make a cottage loaf divide the dough again into one smaller and one larger piece. Put the smaller on top of the larger and then make a hole through the centre of both with a thick wooden skewer.

Put the loaves on a lightly oiled baking sheet and put inside an oiled polythene bag. (This is so much easier than the old method it seems sensible to cheat.) Leave in a warm place for about two hours.

Bake in a preheated oven at 450°F/230°C (Gas Mark 8) for ten minutes, then turn the temperature down to 350°F/180°C (Gas Mark 4) until they sound hollow when tapped. (About 70 minutes).

CURRANT CAKES

Hannell sold his currant cakes at 6d (2½p) per lb, and taking into account the relative values of money, they were slightly more expensive than the price now.

INGREDIENTS:

1 lb (450g) plain flour
7 oz (200g) sugar
1 teaspoon tartaric acid
1 teaspoon bicarbonate of soda
4 oz (115g) butter
4 oz (115g) lard
1 egg
8 oz (225g) currants
1 oz (30g) peel

METHOD: Mix together the flour, sugar, tartaric acid and baking powder.

Rub in the butter and lard.

Add the egg and beat in thoroughly.

Mix in the currants and peel.

Place in a cake tin and bake at 375°F/190°C (Gas Mark 5) for 35 minutes.

Cranford

Lace Makers

Lace making came to this country probably from France in Tudor times and it became a very common cottage industry especially in Northamptonshire, Bedfordshire and Buckinghamshire. Virtually every village in this area had most of its working women engaged in making lace. Once a month would be cutting off day when the lace was taken to one of the big markets such as Daventry or Northampton. There they would sell the lace to an agent who would pay the ladies for their work and sell them bobbins and thread so getting some of his money back. He would also give them a token which could be exchanged for a beer. There is a story of one mother who sent her young daughter to market to sell the lace with strict instructions not to collect the beer token but to get extra bobbins and thread instead.

After the invention of the lace-making machine this cottage industry continued for a short while but by the middle of the nineteenth century it had virtually stopped.

Lace makers had one of two patron saints, many in Northamptonshire celebrated St Andrew's Day which became known as 'Tanders Day' while the rest celebrated St Catherine's Day. There are traditional foods associated with each of these saints' days such as the Tanders cakes which were sliced, spread with butter and eaten with a cup of tea while the others had their Cattern cakes. (Cattern is a corruption of Catherine.) It was traditional for them to eat rabbit casserole and drink the Cattern bowl (see drinks).

Lacemaking school

TANDERS CAKES

INGREDIENTS:

½ teaspoon dried yeast
1 lb (450g) plain flour
½ teaspoon salt
1 teaspoon granulated sugar
½ pint (280ml) warm water
1 egg
4 oz (115g) lard
4 oz (115g) currants
4 oz (115g) castor sugar
1 oz (30g) crystallised lemon peel, diced

METHOD: Dissolve the granulated sugar in the water, add the yeast, and leave in a warm place until it is bubbling actively (15 to 20 mins).

Put the lard in a warm place to soften it.

Beat the egg in a large mixing bowl.

Gradually sift in the flour and mix thoroughly.

Add the activated yeast and continue mixing.

Mix the salt, sugar and warmed lard in with the flour and beat really thoroughly until it has an even texture.

Cover the bowl with a damp cloth and leave in a warm place until it has doubled in size. (A much easier modern way of doing this is to place the dough in a sealed polythene bag.)

Add the currants and diced peel and knead the mixture thoroughly for a minute.

Well grease a 2 lb (1kg) loaf tin.

Put the dough in it and leave in a warm place until it fills the tin.

Bake at 350°F/180°C (Gas Mark 4) until it sounds hollow when tapped. This will be about one hour.

Turn out onto a wire tray to cool.

Slice and serve with butter while still warm – heaven.

RABBIT CASSEROLE

(Serves 4)

INGREDIENTS:

4 rabbit joints
8 oz (225g) cooked ham (thickly sliced)
2 medium carrots
8 small shallots
1 pint (570ml) milk
5 teaspoons salt
Black pepper
¼ teaspoon grated nutmeg
Fresh parsley (optional)
½ oz (15g) corn flour
½ oz (15g) butter

METHOD: Wash the rabbit portions and place them in a casserole dish.

Peel the carrots and shallots, slice them and add to the casserole.

Dice the ham and put this in the casserole together with the milk.

Sprinkle with salt, pepper, grated nutmeg and add a sprig of parsley if liked.

Cook at 350°F/180°C (Gas Mark 4) for an hour.

Drain the liquid into a saucepan and thicken with corn flour.

Add the butter and simmer for three minutes.

Arrange the rabbit portions on a plate, pour over the sauce and garnish with parsley.

CATTERN CAKES

INGREDIENTS:

9 oz (255g) self raising flour
¼ teaspoon ground cinnamon
1 oz (30g) currants
2 oz (55g) ground almonds
2 teaspoons caraway seeds
7 oz (200g) castor sugar
4 oz (115g) melted butter
1 medium egg

METHOD: Put the flour cinnamon, currants, almonds, caraway seeds and sugar into a mixing bowl.

Gently warm the butter until it is melted, then add this to the mixture and stir.

Beat the egg add this to the flour and thoroughly mix to a soft dough.

Roll out on a floured board to give a rectangle about 12 in x 10 in. (30cm x 25cm)

Brush the dough with water then sprinkle it with a little sugar and cinnamon.

Roll the pastry like a swiss roll and cut into slices about 0.8 in (2cm) thick.

Place them well spaced out on a greased baking tray and bake for ten minutes at 400°F/200°C (Gas Mark 6).

Cool on a rack and sprinkle with extra caraway seeds if preferred.

The Waterways of Northamptonshire

Three major rivers have their sources in Northamptonshire. The Avon flows westwards past Shakespeare's birthplace to Tewkesbury where it joins the Severn. This is not navigable in Northamptonshire. The other two are: the Welland which flows eastwards through Stamford and Spalding to The Wash, and the Nene which also flows to The Wash through Peterborough and Wisbech. Even before the building of the canals these were important waterways used for the transport of bulky materials, but then in the late eighteenth and early nineteenth centuries the canal system was developed. This became a major feature of Northamptonshire life. The main canal from London to the Midlands was built to pass through the Watford gap. Later, in 1927, when it was amalgamated with other canals, it became known as the Grand Union Canal.

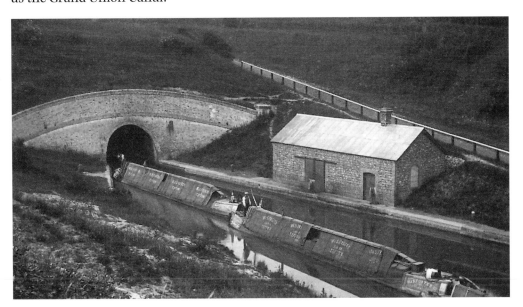

The tunnel, Stoke Bruerne

The narrowboats were able to carry enormous loads and still be kept moving at a steady pace with very little effort. This made them ideal for transporting large non-perishable cargoes. Some of the narrowboats were fitted with sails and when the wind was in the right direction the horses could be brought on board and they would be sailed along the waterway.

Life on the Narrowboats

With two rivers and a major canal system, Northamptonshire is rich in waterways and in the days before the railways they were a very important means of transport, worked by the barge people who lived and brought up families in the confines of the living quarters on their narrow boats. The kitchen area housed a tiny range and was clearly unsuitable for preparing complex meals.

Pay for bargees was poor. It depended on the total weight of the cargo and the distance it was moved. To make a reasonable living they had to work many hours each day, typically starting at 5 a.m. in the morning when the horses were made ready by the bargee while his wife cooked the bacon breakfast. By 6 a.m. they would be under way and would not stop for twelve or fourteen hours, during which time the kettle would be kept permanently on the stove supplying endless cups of tea, which the wife would pass to her husband on the bank. They did not even stop for lunch which would have been perhaps a cheese sandwich or maybe a lump of cold beef eaten as they worked. When they did finally stop they would have a cooked tea or treat themselves to fish and chips, and some would spend the evening in a pub.

Before each voyage they would stock up with food which had to remain edible for the duration of the trip. Bacon was popular, as was cooked beef, and it was traditional for them to take on board a score (20 lb) joint of cooked beef, a large cheese and various vegetables such as potatoes, carrots, parsnips and leeks – apparently barge people would not use onions if they could get hold of leeks.

Sunday was the only day they rested and lunch on that day was the main meal of the week, but even this had to be cooked simply. 'Lobby' short for 'lobscouse' which was a traditional dish for sailors, had been adopted by the barge people as had that old cockney favourite 'Boiled Beef and Carrots'.

LOBBY

Lobscouse was originally a German dish made with fish, but recipes have to adapt and the British sailors changed it to boiled beef, and it is this which was eaten by the barge people.

INGREDIENTS:

1 lb (450g) slices of cooked beef
  (silverside is ideal)
1 lb (450g) onions
6 oz (170g) carrots
3 oz (85g) parsnips
3 oz (85g) swede
1½ lb (680g) potatoes

METHOD: Peel and coarsely slice the onions

Peel the rest of the vegetables and cut them into slices about ⅛ inch (3-4mm) thick.

Put a layer of potatoes on the bottom of a large casserole dish and place on top of this the following layers: onion, beef, mixed root vegetables, potato, mixed root vegetables, beef, onion and finally potato.

Pack the layers as close as possible.

Pour into the casserole sufficient beef stock to almost cover the top layer of potato.

Place the lid on the casserole and leave in a preheated oven at 250°F/121°C (Gas Mark ½) for two and a half to three hours.

Lobby is easy to prepare because it is a complete meal cooked in one container but the best thing about it is the flavour. This one is a real joy to eat.

BOILED BEEF AND CARROTS

(Serves 2)

This meal must be made with cooked beef, so if all you have is raw meat then cut it into bite sized pieces and place it in boiling water for long enough to thoroughly seal it. The advantage of using cooked meat is that the gravy remains clear; clear gravy and lots of it is the secret of this meal, so when everything else has been eaten it can be mopped up with a couple of slices of good thick bread.

INGREDIENTS: *To make the casserole*
12 oz (340g) cooked beef
6 oz (170g) carrots
2 medium leeks
4 oz (115g) turnips, parsnips and/or swede as available
A stick of celery (optional)

To make the dumplings
2 oz (55g) self raising flour
1 oz (30g) shredded suet
A pinch of salt
Water

METHOD: Cut the beef into bite sized pieces and place in a casserole.

Peel and slice the carrots, cut the celery stick into approximately ½ inch (1cm) lengths and dice the remaining vegetables, putting them all in the casserole.

Place the casserole in an oven at 250°F/120°C (Gas Mark ½) for two hours.

While it is cooking place the flour, suet and salt in a mixing bowl and mix in a little water very gradually until it has the consistency of dough.

Break the dough into four equal sized pieces and roll into balls on a floured board

After the casserole has been cooking for about one and a half hours, add the dumplings and cook for a further one and a half hours.

Serve this dish with boiled potatoes and a couple of slices of dry bread per person.

The Whitworth Brothers

The Whitworth Brothers; John, Herbert and Newton, had been born into what was a substantial farming and milling family. Together in 1886 they started a milling business on the banks of the River Nene at Wellingborough. Their mill was powered by steam and used rollers rather than millstones to crush the wheat, which at that time was in the forefront of technology. Theirs was the first roller mill in the country, though its success ensured that they were soon copied by others.

The choice of site on the Nene was a good one as they were able to use narrow boats for their bulky transportation, and such boats were still in use up to 1969.

It was one of the original founders, John B. Whitworth, who in the 1930s bought the then ailing Weetabix company and turned it into the successful Burton Latimer factory which though now no longer part of Whitworth's is still supplied by them.

The Embankment, Wellingborough

After the Second World War Whitworth Bros. expanded their interests in packaging techniques and once again led the way, this time in the supply of convenience foods. They became especially well known for washing and packaging dried fruits which might not seem unusual today but at that time it was a big improvement over the sale of unwashed, gritty dried fruits that had to be weighed out by the shopkeeper whenever they were required.

The packaging part of the business was sold off in 1988 and the company known as 'Whitworths Limited' in Irthlingborough continues this operation as a completely separate organisation.

As for Whitworth Bros Ltd, it is a friendly group which continues supplying flour and cereals to many of this country's largest bakers and breakfast cereal manufacturers and they still do it from the same site on the banks of the Nene where they started all those years ago.

Canal tunnel, Blisworth

Pub Life in the Mid-Nineteenth Century

It was in the 1860s that gas started to be supplied to houses, and gas lighting even with all its difficulties was a big improvement over candles. The astute publican who had gaslight fitted had an environment where people could spend the evening in the light. They would have a big fire in the hearth and the customers would sit around this with a quartern loaf supplied by the publican (A quartern is a quarter of a stone = 3½ lb. It is said that these loaves had salt added to the dough to make their customers thirstier). The customers would sit by the fire toasting and buttering the bread (with salted butter of course). Some people would bring a steak or chop along for the publican to cook while they would sit, chat and drink the ale brought to them, probably from the tap room. Public houses in those days were rather like peoples' homes and they would sit round the fire rather than at the bar.

The Bee's Wing, Sheep Street, Wellingborough

Chapter 11

TRADITIONAL HOME COOKING

In this section recipes have been included for various reasons. Some require the use of specific implements, some are ways to use up scraps, while others are special foods for invalids.

It has been estimated that in 1806, 50% more butter, veal and pork was produced in Northamptonshire than was needed to feed its population. These surpluses were transported to London where they were sold. At that time the farmland of Northamptonshire was about equally divided between grazing land and grass crops. Cattle were brought in from areas of poorer grazing to be fattened prior to slaughter so it comes as little surprise that they had a surplus of milk which was impossible for them to keep and their solution was to turn it into butter, but this created the by-products skimmed milk and butter milk.

The first stage of butter production is to separate the cream from the rest of the milk, leaving skimmed milk. In those days when whole milk was sold for 3d a pint, the skimmed milk only cost 1d, unlike today when there is no such price differential.

The next stage in butter making is to churn the cream until the fat and protein coagulate together to make the butter, which is removed leaving behind the sweet watery liquid called butter milk. It was considered to be a refreshing drink, and as it contained sugar it probably did refresh them, but it was not everyone who enjoyed this rather watery drink, and no doubt they were pleased to find other uses for it.

Another by-product of the milk industry is calves because a cow only produces milk after she has had a calf, and it is not therefore surprising that veal too was overproduced in this county.

High Street, Gayton

BUTTERMILK SCONES

24 scones

This is a typical recipe for using up the surplus buttermilk and this ensured that as little as possible went to waste.

INGREDIENTS:
1 lb (450g) plain flour
1 oz (30g) butter
A good pinch of salt
1 heaped teaspoon bicarbonate of soda
1 level teaspoon cream of tartar
½ pint (280ml) buttermilk

METHOD: Sift the flour into a mixing bowl and add the salt, bicarbonate of soda and cream of tartar, then rub the butter into the flour.

Gradually mix in the buttermilk until the dough is fairly soft but not sticky.

Roll out the dough on a floured surface and cut into about two dozen rounds, and cook on a hot well-floured griddle for about four minutes each side. However, 12 to 15 minutes in a preheated oven at 425°F/220°C (Gas Mark 7) should do just as well.

BUTTERMILK BREAD

The same recipe as for the scones except that the dough is not cut into rounds but rolled into a ball. Two cuts are made with a sharp knife at right angles to each other across the top of the dough. This is placed on a floured baking sheet, sprinkled with flour and baked at 425°F/220°C (Gas Mark 7) for 25 to 30 minutes.

RAMEKINS

INGREDIENTS:
4 oz (115g) hard cheese
2 raw whites of eggs
1 oz (30g) butter
4 slices of bread

METHOD: Beat the cheese, butter and uncooked egg whites in a mortar until it is smooth and like a thick slightly frothy cream.

Toast the bread.

Spread the mixture over it.

Brown the top with a salamander.

This is a version of Welsh rarebit which comes from a Northamptonshire notebook written around 1815. In the absence of a grill they used an iron which was heated and used to brown the tops of pies and the like to give them a pleasant appearance. The salamander was the precursor of the waffle iron.

Market Place, Long Buckby, 10 March 1907

GRAVY SOUP

INGREDIENTS: **1 shin of beef**
1 head of celery
1 onion
A bunch of sweet herbs
Various vegetables as available

METHOD: Soak the shin in boiling water to seal it then place in the digester.

Add all the other ingredients and cover with water.

Leave it by the side of the fire for a whole day.

The next morning skim off the fat.

If the soup is not clear strain it through a cloth.

Wash and replace the vegetables in the soup, heat and serve when required.

The lid should be on the digester all the time the gravy is cooking.

This recipe comes from Wootton Hall and dates from about 1850. It requires the use of a digester, which is a saucepan with a tightly fitting lid that allows the pressure inside the saucepan to rise. This early form of pressure cooker was invented by Denis Papin in about 1675. By boiling bones in the digester a jelly was produced which was considered to be a very good food for invalids. The digester could be left by the side of the fire all day if necessary. It was used to stew food for very long times and to soften cheap cuts of meat.

SAUSAGE AND APPLE PIE

(Serves 4)

INGREDIENTS: **8 oz (225g) short crust pastry**
2 cooking apples
1 lb (450g) pork sausage meat
Chutney

METHOD: Line a 7½-inch. (38cm) tin with the pastry. Leave enough pastry for the lid.

Spread a layer of chutney thinly over the base.

Put the sausage meat in the pie.

Core and peel the apples, slice thinly and place them over the meat.

Cover with pastry in the usual way by moistening the edges of the pastry and pinching them together.

Cook at 375°F/190°C (Gas Mark 5) for one and a half hours.

Serve hot with vegetables or cold with salad.

Mill Lane, Old Duston, 1920

One of the arts of cooking in a less affluent household was to produce something that appeared to be a meaty meal using a minimum of meat. Sausages are a good example of this, but then to make the little bit of meat in the sausages go even further they might come up with something like sausage and apple pie.

STEWED GREEN PEAS

INGREDIENTS:
1 lb (450g) fresh peas
1 lettuce
1 onion
2 oz (55g) butter, pepper and salt
1 tablespoon of water
1 egg
½ teaspoon icing sugar

METHOD: Cut the onion and lettuce into slices and put in a large saucepan with the peas.

Add the butter, salt, pepper and tablespoon of water to the saucepan.

Put the lid on the saucepan and stew very gently for one hour.

Beat the eggs and sugar together. Add this to the saucepan and heat gently, without boiling, until it thickens.

This recipe comes from the recipes of Mrs Fermor (c1865) and has been included for its rather unusual way of treating lettuce.

Castle Ashby

NORTHAMPTONSHIRE CHEESE CAKES

This recipe comes from the Barby W.I. and was taken from the *Northamptonshire Federation of Women's Institutes' Recipe Book*. 5th Edn. Notably it is made from milk which is clotted rather than ready made curd cheese. In the same book there is a similar recipe from the Crick W. I. and they claim it is peculiar to Northamptonshire and Leicestershire.

INGREDIENTS:

2 oz (55g) butter
3 oz (85g) sugar
4 oz (115g) currants
2 eggs
2 pints (1.1 litres) milk
Almond essence to taste
Grated rind of 1 lemon
A pinch of ground nutmeg
1 dessertspoon vinegar

METHOD: Beat the eggs well and mix them with the butter and sugar in a saucepan.

Warm gently until thick but not curdish.

In a separate saucepan boil the milk to which a dessertspoonful of vinegar has been added.

Stop heating when it separates into curds and whey, then strain and leave to cool.

Add the currants, grated lemon rind and spices to the cold curds and mix thoroughly with the previously thickened mixture of butter, sugar and eggs.

Pour this into pastry tins lined with pastry and bake at 425°F/220°C (Gas Mark 7) for 20 minutes.

BRIGSTOCK PICKLE

This recipe comes from the Brigstock W.I. and was taken from the *Northamptonshire Federation of Women's Institutes' Recipe Book* 5th Edn.

INGREDIENTS:

**4 lb (1.8kg) mixed diced vegetables
(vegetable marrow, green tomatoes,
onions, apples, small kidney beans and
cauliflower)
¼ teaspoon salt
2 dessertspoons sugar
2 pints (1.1 litres) vinegar
1 tablespoon flour
1 level teaspoon mustard
1 level teaspoon turmeric**

METHOD: Cut the vegetables into small pieces.

Sprinkle over the salt and sugar then cover with vinegar.

Leave to stand for twelve hours.

Boil until the vegetables are soft then mix the flour, mustard and turmeric to a paste with a little vinegar and add to the vegetables.

Boil the mixture until it thickens (about three minutes).

Put into jars and seal when cold.

Brigstock, 1907

A GOOD NORTHAMPTONSHIRE PUDDING

This is the last recipe taken from the *Northamptonshire Federation of Women's Institutes' Recipe Book* (5th Ed.) It was submitted by the Cogenhoe W. I.

INGREDIENTS: **2 oz (55g) butter**
4 oz (115g) self-raising flour
3 oz (85g) castor sugar
2 eggs
1 tablespoon raspberry jam

METHOD: Cream together the butter and sugar.

Let it stand for 15 minutes

Add the flour and eggs alternately.

Mix in the jam.

Place in a pudding basin, cover and steam for two hours.

Cogenhoe Mill

APPLE PIE

What more traditional home cooking could there be than apple pie?

'Apple Pie' by A. Adcock, *Northamptonshire County Magazine*, Vol. 1, p. 56 (1928).

Dear Nelly, learn with care the pastry art,
And mind the easy percepts I impart:
Draw out your dough elaborately thin,
And cease not to fatigue your rolling pin:
Of eggs and butter see you mix enough:
For then the paste will swell into a puff,

Reng'd in thick order let your quinces lie;
They give a charming relish to the pie.
If you are wise, you'll not brown sugar slight,
The browner (If I form my judgement right)
A deep vermilion tincture will dispense,
And make your pippin redder than the quince.

When this is done, there will be wanting still,
The just reserve of cloves and candied peel
Nor can I blame you, if a drop you take
Of orange-water, for perfuming sake.
But here the nicety of art is such,
There must not be too little nor too much,

To choose your baker, think, and think again
(You'll scarce one honest baker find in ten):
Adust and bruis'd, I've often seen a pie,
In rich disguise and costly ruin lie,
Then shalt thou, pleas'd the noble fabric view,
And have a slice into the bargain too;
Honour and fame alike we will partake,
So well I'll eat what you so richly make.

Chapter 12

LIFE IN BYGONE NORTHAMPTONSHIRE

In medieval Northamptonshire there were numerous villages where each person had their own allocation of land and managed it by what was then the traditional ridge and furrow method. This gave the land a gently rolling appearance, like the waves in mid-ocean, and this can still be seen in several places in Northamptonshire today; for example, Abington Park in Northampton. They ploughed the land using oxen and a ploughshare the design of which hardly changed until the twentieth century. Of course in many ways the life of the medieval farmers would have been strange to us, for example they would not have had rabbits in their diet because these were not introduced into England until after the Norman invasion but there would have been a good supply of freshwater fish from the village fishpond which would have been dug as a communal project. These ponds were stocked with fish such as carp and were an important source of food, especially on Fridays when the eating of meat was forbidden by the church. Fishponds were often associated with monasteries or priories like those at Chacombe and Weedon, but probably most medieval villages also had them. Evidence of village fishponds can still be found in many places in Northamptonshire such as Charwelton, Collyweston and Paulerspury. Indeed it was not uncommon for these ponds to be constructed in pairs as at Holcot. It seems that they had quite a sophisticated system of fish farming at Silverstone where there was a whole series of ponds.

Many of the place names we have in Northamptonshire date back to medieval times and these often provide an insight into the past. In Northampton 'Greyfriars' was once the site of a monastery while 'Mayor Hold' is the place where the mares were held separate from the stallions prior to being sold at 'Mairfair'.

The names of some areas in the county give an insight into the food that was associated with them. Obvious examples are 'Apple Tree' in Aston-le-Walls, 'Honey Hill' in Cold Ashby, 'Orchard Hill' at Little Billing and Oxendon presumably was once famous for its oxen. The suffix 'pury' indicates pears and presumably these were grown at Paulerspury and Potterspury. It is not an accident that so many of the examples given above refer to orchards as the towns and villages throughout Northamptonshire had numerous orchards; the cherry orchards of Northampton and the nut orchards of Newnham were particularly famous in their day.

In Tudor times there were to be important changes in land ownership. The first moves towards land enclosure were taking place. This was an attempt to take land away from common ownership and allow it to become the property of individual Landowners. At the start of Henry VIII's reign the church owned almost half the land in England, but Henry seized it by force and sold it off cheaply to people who were already wealthy. Almost all of the numerous stately homes in Northamptonshire were initially built in Tudor times. In each village there would be several people trying to make a living with small amounts of common land while the Lord of the Manor owned the majority and best of the land.

Dovecotes were a feature of Northamptonshire in Tudor times and there are several still remaining in the county, such as those at Islip, Duddington and the especially famous one at Collyweston which is dated 1578. Traditionally it was only the Lord of the Manor who was allowed to have a dovecote because he would not want other people's doves (pigeons) taking the grain from his land. However, it was not uncommon for him to allow the Vicar to have a dovecote too. Having achieved a privileged position in this world the Lord of the Manor would not want to spoil his chances in the next by getting on the wrong side of God's ambassador.

Northamptonshire has an enormous number of natural springs and because of the iron-rich nature of the bedrock it is not surprising that the spring water was chalybeate (rich in iron). The spa at Bath had been particularly successful and in Northamptonshire there were several attempts to develop spas commercially. There was Fincheswell at Cosgrove, Redwell at Wellingborough and St Loy's (St Lucien's) at Weedon. Of all these it was the spa at Astrop that was most successful; it functioned for nearly a hundred years and included royalty among its patrons.

By Victorian times there had inevitably been some developments in agricultural methods, but bigger changes were to come. In the hundred years following 1850 there would be more significant changes than in the whole of the thousand years before.

By 1850 the first recipe book to give practical details of quantities and cooking times had only recently been published. Mrs Beaton had yet to publish her famous book and this would be followed by a multitude of other recipe books making recipes available to all and so hastening the decline of regional cooking.

By 1850 the enclosure of land was virtually complete and a few wealthy people had benefited from it while the poor had lost an important means of support for their family. The industrial revolution had largely bypassed Northamptonshire and so the majority of the poor had little choice but to work as farm labourers and this work was notoriously poorly paid.

The Corn Laws restricting the importation of cereals had been introduced to keep the price grain high, and they were in effect from 1815 to 1845. During that time the price of flour became too high for the poor farm labourers, and potatoes became their staple diet. The spread of potato blight across Europe brought the end of the Corn Laws but it also took away their staple food. The importation of cheap grain brought down the cost of bread but it also reduced the farmers' profits and this inevitably affected farm labourers' wages. These were hard times for the poor of Northamptonshire but in this 'land of squires and spires', where there was a higher proportion of gentry than in any other county of England there was, as always, a big discrepancy between the rich and the poor. It was not uncommon for a wealthy family of half a dozen to have ten times that number of servants taking care of them. The poor were only too happy to see their sons and daughters go into service in the big houses where they would have regular food in exchange for long working hours.

As in Tudor times the two most influential people in the village were the Lord of the Manor and the Vicar. There would be various tradespeople – the butcher, the baker and the candlestick maker together with a blacksmith, shoemakers, farmers and farm labourers, brewers and publicans. Typically a village would have two or three pubs and one church. (Denominations other than Church of England were by now beginning to build their own churches or chapels so some villages might have more than one place of public worship and the large estates might also have their own family church.) The butcher and baker would each have their own shop and there would be at least one general store.

Most of the villagers spent virtually the whole of their lives in the village. Living and working together they came to know each other very well. The carrier with his horse and cart was for them an important connection with the outside world and he would bring various necessities into the village. Another feature of the Victorian village would be the local school. The long summer holidays that our children enjoy today are a relic of the long summer holidays they had in Victorian times when even the children had to help with the harvest.

So what would life have been like in a typical Northamptonshire village one day in 1850? While the rest of the village slept, the poacher might be out and about. He would want to catch as many animals as possible and probably have them skinned and gutted before the rest of the village was awake. If he had a good night he might have enough animals to take to market and he would certainly want to be on his way before anyone started asking awkward questions about where they came from. The next person to get up in the village was the baker. He would probably be up by about four in the morning so as to have fresh bread for the farm labourers to take to work. Being enterprising, as it seems most bakers were, he might also sell fruit from his garden and maybe some other sideline like tobacco which the farm labourers would smoke in a short clay pipe. In the big houses the kitchen maid might also be up at about four so that she too could bake bread for the household's breakfast. On the river, bargees would start to move at about six o'clock, while the farm labourers might not have to go to work until around seven-thirty. Gradually the rest of the village would wake up and, by about half past nine, breakfast would be being served in the stately home.

It was the job of the Victorian wife to see that her husband remained fit, and no man could be expected to do a day's work and remain healthy if he did not have a good breakfast. Breakfast was considered to be an important meal by rich and poor alike. A farm labourer might get yesterday's leftovers before he went to work, whereas in the big house a typical breakfast would include bacon, boiled eggs, toast and perhaps cooked mushrooms together with several meat and poultry dishes. These could include cold dishes such as potted meats, pork pies and brawn or hot dishes such as sheep's brains, toasted bone marrow, partridge, rump steak and many more. Kedgeree was a particular favourite at this time, as were kromeskies (cromeskies). If they had visitors staying overnight then breakfast would be even more lavish. Tea and coffee were not widely drunk at breakfast, and in the big houses cocoa would be the most common breakfast drink. The biggest houses would have a separate breakfast room and the various pies and cold meats would be left there until well into the morning so that anyone who was a little late getting up could still help themselves to a meal. If the wealthy rose early it would probably be to go shooting or trapping and they would expect an early breakfast before they left and another on their return. The second breakfast would have been much the same as the first but with the addition of considerable quantities of beer and wine.

Lunch meant very different things to different people. For the baker it often marked the end of his working day. After lunch his wife might sell bread in their shop but he would have no more baking to do and he might relax by tending his garden during the afternoon. Many other workers would be able to get home for lunch, for example the blacksmith who almost invariably lived next to the forge. For him lunch would be a welcome break from work. The shadiest, coolest tree is the chestnut and these were commonly planted near the smithy, but even in its shade the blacksmith's work was hot and exhausting and his lunch would probably include a few beers to replace the fluid he lost in perspiration.

KEDGEREE

This curried dish became popular when India was part of the British Empire. Along with many other dishes it shows the influence of foreign food on our British cuisine. Kedgeree was enormously popular in Victorian Northamptonshire.

INGREDIENTS:

4 hard boiled eggs
12 oz (340g) boiled haddock.
  (Other boiled white fish such as turbot, sole or pike were also used)
1 oz (25g) butter
Salt, cayenne pepper and curry powder.

METHOD: Boil the rice until thoroughly cooked then drain.

Chop the hard-boiled eggs and add them to the rice.

Cut the cooked fish into small pieces and remove any bones.

Melt the butter in a large pan and add all the other ingredients.

Cook steadily with constant stirring until thoroughly heated and serve hot.

Barry Road School, Northampton, 1912

The farm labourers would not go home for lunch. They would have a packed lunch in the fields; it might be sandwiches, a pie or even a clanger. The farmer would provide ale (probably short beer) for his labourers and in this way they would be fortified during the long days of harvesting.

The bargees would eat a cold lunch while they worked, as did their counterparts on land, the carriers. These men would probably have a pack of sandwiches or a pie to eat as they drove although it was not unknown for carriers to stop at one or more of the alehouses along their route and occasionally only manage to get home because the horse knew the way back. There is one story of a Northamptonshire carrier whose horse would not move until he came out of the pub and climbed up onto the cart, then the horse would make its way home without any further word of command. One day this carrier appears to have fallen sleep and then fallen from his cart. It seems that he continued to sleep by the roadside while the horse made its way home unaided.

On market day people would go to town to sell whatever they could. Cows, horses, pigs, ducks, geese, etc. would all be taken to market and the farm hands who took them would spend some of their wages in the many ale houses that remained open all day.

The men from the big houses would probably be out at business, or perhaps hunting. When hunting they would take some food with them in case the chase did not take them by a pub. The huntsmen would have pies and sandwiches specially prepared so that they were firm enough to withstand the buffeting they received during the chase.

In the big house, luncheon would be a meal for the ladies. They would eat cold meats, pies, sweet puddings and fruits. A classic dish for luncheon was the galantine which consisted of four or five layers of various meats and stuffing rolled in a cloth and cooked in boiling stock. A recipe for a simple beef galantine is given on page 171. Various local ladies would drop in for luncheon but it was considered bad form for them to stay much longer than a quarter of an hour and it would have been a serious breech of etiquette for them to take off their coat or hat. They sat in their outdoor clothes eating food which had to be dainty and not too messy.

KROMESKIES

Kromeskies are the Polish version of the croquette; they were popular in the big houses throughout England.

INGREDIENTS: *Filling*

**8 oz (225g) cooked chicken
   or turkey breast**
2 oz (55g) cooked ham
5 fl oz (140ml.) stock
1 oz (30g) butter
1 oz (30g) flour
1 tablespoon cream
1 teaspoon lemon juice
6 button mushrooms
1 truffle
Salt and pepper to taste

Coat

2 fl oz (55ml) milk
1 oz (55g) butter
4 oz (110g) flour
1 large egg
**About ten rashers of smoked
   streaky bacon**
Salt

METHOD: Chop the chicken, ham, mushrooms and truffle finely.

Gently warm the flour in the butter until it has all been absorbed.

Slowly add the stock with gentle heating to make a roux.

Add the chopped ingredients, cream, lemon juice, salt and pepper and stir together.

Roll into croquettes.

To make the batter rub the butter into the flour and add the salt.

Beat the egg and thoroughly mix it into the flour.

Gradually add the milk mixing all the time to make a smooth batter.

Wrap a rasher of bacon around each croquette, dip in the batter and deep fry.

BEEF GALANTINE

INGREDIENTS:
1 lb (450g) beef stewing steak.
8 oz (225g) breadcrumbs
1 lb (450g) raw ham
2 large eggs
Mace, nutmeg, salt and pepper
2 pints (1.1 litres) beef stock

METHOD: Mince the steak and finely chop the ham.

Beat the eggs and mix in all the other ingredients except the stock.

Roll the mixture into a large sausage shape.

Wrap in a pudding cloth and tie to hold it together.

Put the stock in a large saucepan and heat until boiling, add the galantine and reduce the heat to simmer for two and a half hours.

The galantine should remain submerged in the stock throughout.

After cooking remove the galantine from the stock and place it on a dish, invert another plate over it and weight it down.

Galantines were often glazed and ornamented before serving cold.

Around five o'clock the Lady of the big house would take tea. She had entertained casual acquaintances at luncheon and might even have allowed her children to come to see her, but teatime was reserved for closer friends. These ladies would be invited to attend her 'at home' (men would avoid the teas as assiduously as they did the luncheons). Tea would be served buffet style and would consist of sandwiches, cakes, scones, biscuits and fruits. Tea (the drink) would be served and this was such an important feature that the meal was named after it. Tea was considered to be a potent drug and was not usually consumed earlier in the day. Wine and even sherry might also be served, but the main ingredient was gossip together with occasional helpings of planning and plotting.

SCONES

INGREDIENTS:

1 dessertspoon of baking powder
1 teaspoon of salt
2 lb (900g) flour
12 oz (340g) butter
4 eggs
1 pint (570ml) milk

METHOD: Beat the eggs and mix them with the milk

Rub the butter into the other ingredients then add the milk and mix thoroughly.

Roll into a disc about ½ inch (13mm) thick.

Score across the dough (like a Union Jack) so that when cooked it can be broken into eight pieces.

Bake at 400°F/200°C (Gas Mark 6) for up to 20 minutes.

During harvest time when the wife, too, would be out in the fields, it was the stockpot that was the easiest way to prepare a nourishing meal, with perhaps a slice or two of bread to mop up the gravy. Some would take their meat down to the local pub and have it cooked there. When there were several pubs in a village each would cater for a particular trade, and people would go to them according to the work they did even to the extent of walking past a more nearby pub.

Dinner in the big houses was quite elaborate; it would be served at about eight o'clock and even if only the immediate family were present it would consist of several courses. If they were entertaining, then dinner would be a very grand affair with a minimum of seven courses, such as soup, fish, roast meat or poultry, sweet pudding (perhaps jelly), cheese and fruits, and there would be several choices for each course and also a good selection of wines. After dinner the men would withdraw to another room. The lady of the house might only see her husband during the day at breakfast and dinner.

The last meal of the day was supper. Before they went to bed the working families would have something to eat, if only a piece of bread. In the big houses the fashion for large and late dinners brought about the decline of their traditional supper which in former days would have been a substantial meal consisting perhaps of bread and butter, poached eggs, cold meat, cold pies, fruit and jelly. It would take a robust character to tackle that after one of their elaborate dinners. However, a snack of oysters and celery might be welcomed. The oysters were expected to stimulate certain appetites and it was believed that the celery would help the man when it came to fulfilling the oyster's promise.

Near Woodford Mill, Thrapston

Until the publication of this book there had not been a collection of traditional Northamptonshire recipes. Bringing them together has been a very pleasurable task both for the food and the insights into the lifestyles of our predecessors. I hope that you too have enjoyed it.